The Letters

Some How It'll Never End

SYDNEY MCBRIDE

Full Circle Publishing

Books may be purchased by contacting the publisher and author at:
www.SomeHowItllNeverEnd.com

Full Circle Publishing
Orlando, Florida

First Edition
Printed in the United States of America

Library of Congress Control Number: 2015913498

ISBN: 978-1494856878
ISBN: 1494856875

For the believers.

Psalm 18:39

CONTENTS

AUTHOR'S NOTE

The following collection of letters was written from 2007-2012, over the five years that I owned a small business, a cheerleading gym- Shine Athletics.

In May of 2012, I made the decision to merge Shine Athletics together with another cheerleading program in hopes to create a larger, super gym program that would offer cheerleading along with multiple other children's activities. Prior to the merger, I had a huge end of the year banquet for all of the Shine athletes and their families to celebrate our journey and milestones over the course of the five years.

At the end of the banquet, I gave all of the athletes and their families printed copies of a compilation of letters I had written over the years. I bound all of the pages together, put a title of "The Letters" on the first page, and put a plastic cover sheet on the front to make it look official.

These letters were personal stories of hopes, dreams, motivation, and lessons I had learned throughout the five years I built and grew Shine Athletics. I would write them to the athletes prior to big competitions or events and then give them to them to read as a good luck charm before they competed. All of the letters and stories are very close to my heart and personal. So much, that I really never intended to share them with the world. However, I always knew that Shine was a very special gift from above that I got to share with so many people, it only made sense that the story had to be shared as well. I vowed to write the entire story down, in a more detailed format than just binding together copies of letters I had written throughout the years.

When I sat down to actually write it all down and finally put this story on paper, I fully intended to have pages and pages of flowing text easily spill out of me so I could write it all in a regular story format for everyone to read.

However, I didn't.

I got so frustrated that I couldn't get the story to flow out of me and fill the pages I was trying to write. How was I going to share this story if I couldn't even figure out which format to use? Every time I would write a page, I would go back to the compilation of letters and try to incorporate it, or edit it, or change it. I wanted everything to be clear, concise and a format and style that others could enjoy. I purchased so many memoirs to try to study and copy the format and style, I lost count.

What I realized is that I was never going to be able to write a normal story or a normal memoir about something that was never normal at all. I was never going to find a format that every single person could understand.

Old letters written to your teenage cheerleaders? Who would want to read that? People that don't know cheerleading won't even understand it. When I would explain it to others, they would ask who's your audience? How are you going to sell a book like that? What would you even write in a press release?

I questioned myself. I doubted myself, and I closed the file on The Letters.
What if people read it, just to make fun of it?
What if my writing is so horrible, that I ruin my chances of ever writing something else?

I realized that I let my doubt become stronger than my belief.

And in that moment, life came full circle.

Every message I tried to share and teach through running a business that served young athletes would instantly be negated if I allowed my fear of criticism and failure to outweigh my belief that these letters and stories could help motivate someone else to go after what they want and pursue their dreams.

Our slogan at Shine Athletics was "Our belief is stronger than your doubt," and after months of staring at an empty screen and blinking cursor, I realized I had to make a conscious decision to practice what I had preached for so long.

I already had so many beautiful stories through the letters that I had written over the years, that the only format for me to begin telling my story about Shine would be to share what I had already written. Share to remember, to cherish, and to reignite a spark that I had been missing.

I had been so consumed with what other people would think, or read, or not read, that I forgot my original mission years ago. I wrote the letters to build belief. The belief that anything really is possible and the belief that anyone can create a reality with the possibilities they desire. At any age, at any time- it is our stories, our backgrounds, and our beliefs that are meant to drive us forward; not hold us back. Our greatest dreams are always running ahead of us, aren't they? We always want what's next, we always want more, and most people think the end goal is to catch the dream, but only the lucky ones realize that it's not catching the dream but running with the dream that matters.

These pages are a written testament to what it's like to run with a dream, to be engulfed inside of a dream, and to live it fully. They are the truest documentation I have of how things really were and how I really felt. They weren't written for mass publication, they were simply written to speak to young athletes who I was hoping could relate or find some source of hope as they read my words.

The majority of these letters were written late night or very early morning, on a night where I couldn't sleep. The grammar isn't the best and I am well aware of typos and mistakes. But, as I started to try to edit, fix the typos and find all of the mistakes… Something just didn't feel right.

I wanted them to stay original. *The Letters* is the real compilation of the real letters that I wrote at that real moment in time.

At no point did I run a perfect business and at no point do I expect to create a perfect piece of writing work. I am consciously making the choice to not over edit my original work so that as you read, the voice that you hear coming off of the pages isn't fictional, but my own. Every sentence may not be correct, but every sentence is real; and that is what makes these pages sweeter than fiction.

I don't expect everyone to understand the cheerleading terminology used at times, but it is my hope that they can understand the heart and soul behind the story. I pray that the words I have written share a crystal clear picture and the forever proof of how much I loved the audience that I was writing to.

The lessons and the love, the setbacks and the comebacks, and the reflections of growing up are the underlying messages that I hope become the takeaway as you fold back the pages. These words will forever be proof that the things we share are the things we can never lose.

The Letters

FOREWORD
SEASON FIVE
APRIL 2012

The following pages are full of letters, journal entries, quotes, stories, and flashbacks that I have given to cheerleaders at Shine Athletics throughout the past five years. They are the insight on what made Shine Athletics, "Shine."

Everything you read is real and has been given to someone at one time or another. The "Last Letter" is essentially the last letter I chose to write and is specifically geared towards my athletes that are graduating, going to college, in college, or moving on to the next stage of their life. It is my hope that our younger cheerleaders will keep this collection of letters and have it to look back on as they get older. I think all of the stories contained in this compilation can have different meanings during different times of life. Just like seasons change, so do we- and hopefully the insight and motivation is the constant that remains the same as you read.

I didn't ever plan on sharing these memories and moments with everyone, but at the same time- I think the following letters and stories are the things that will live on as the greatest memories of Shine.

Shine was real- it was a struggle and it was so much more than a cheer gym- it was me growing up and it was everything I ever needed it to be.

On April 2, 2007 I signed a five year lease on a warehouse that wasn't built yet and technically didn't exist.

A month later, in May of 2007, we had uniform fittings and cheer team signups at the local public library. Around forty kids came to be a part of this "new" cheer gym.

Due to numerous permitting and construction delays, we were unable to occupy our warehouse and had to rent space at a local middle school to start summer practices. The entire month of June and part of July we practiced in the middle school gymnasium; the very same gymnasium that I spent three years of middle school P.E. Class in, many years prior.

Towards the middle of July- we started practicing in our facility without electricity, air conditioning, or proper permits to occupy the building. Yes, you read that correctly. And now I guess I can openly admit that those first few weeks we practiced without the proper permitting or permission of the contracting company, landlord, and city. Practices had to start at 6pm so I had time (after the construction crews left) to run an extension cord from someone else's power supply to the lights I hung up to use until the power got turned on. (I'm sorry.)

July 27, 2007 the power was switched on and we began official practices in the Shine Athletics facility, with actual permits that made it official.

We had three and a half cheer teams: A small senior age team, a large senior age team, a youth age team, and three five year olds that made up our "tiny" team.

Fast forward to 2012, five years later- Shine Athletics is home to nine all-star cheer teams, a preschool cheer class, over 75 athletes enrolled in rec classes, and held a huge showcase with over 23 cheer teams from across the community.

If someone had told me five years ago that this is where I would be today…. I don't think I would've believed them.

There is so much more to tell and so much that fills in the past five years. I thought I would be the one teaching, but I have been the one who has truly been taught. There have been so many good times, bad times, hard times, and seemingly impossible times.

I have learned how to love, how to win, and most importantly how to lose. I have experienced some of the greatest moments of joy and happiness and some of the lowest moments of failure and pain. I have watched former athletes grow up and move on to the next chapters of their lives and I have also watched kids from the same peer groups succumb to pressure and venture down dark paths. I have seen athletes come back from impossible injuries and overcome the impossible. I have also lived through the greatest heartbreak of all, as I watched as one of my cheerleaders was buried. I have learned the true meaning behind the quote "Success is a journey, not a destination" and I have learned what it is like to truly have a passion and to love something more than anything or anyone else.

When I have time to truly tell the full story and fill in all the blanks of the past five years, I will do it. It will be an amazing book that will explain the back stories behind all of these pages. I'm looking forward to filling in the blanks and I'm looking forward to the next chapter and the next story.

But for now, I leave you with *The Letters.*

SEASON 1 LETTERS

"Every great success is an accumulation of thousands of ordinary efforts that no one sees or appreciates."
                                                        -Brian Tracey

SEASON ONE
SATURDAY, DECEMBER 15, 2007

I'm graduating from college tomorrow.

Wow.

Writing down those words on paper is the only thing that makes it feel real. Shouldn't I feel more anticipation? Where's the celebration to this universally proclaimed success? A college graduation is supposed to be a big deal, right? Maybe what I feel is just different. There will be no celebration, no big family dinner, and no party. Just my Mom in the audience and we will ride home together afterwards. Other than the cap and gown, it is very similar to any other day.

Maybe my lack of feeling like this is a peak moment stems from my excitement surrounding the day after graduation.

They say every new beginning comes from some other beginning's end; and in this case, that quote couldn't be more accurate.

Tomorrow, I will walk inside my college arena and mark the finale of my college career. Sunday, one day after, I will walk back inside the same arena and mark an entirely new beginning.

Sunday is my very first all-star cheer competition that I will be attending as a coach, as a gym owner, and with the responsibility of four teams of cheerleaders. In less than 24 hours after graduation, I am officially a full time working adult. I skipped all of the resume building workshops, the last semester internship, and the interview 101 classes. I've been going to school every day this last semester, only to drive straight to the gym to coach cheerleading. I think part of me is relieved, relieved to have a break from going to school and working at the same time. Now I can truly devote my entire focus to growing the cheer program.

Milestones, like graduation, make me look back and reflect. Reflecting makes the dots connect. The big decisions we debate over for weeks and the small, even tiniest choices we make that seem so unimportant along the way.... They all melt together to bring us to our present.

Sometimes I pinch myself, worried that this isn't real. Am I going to wake up and find myself at the first day of college all over again? Am I really finally done?

The next two days are really just proof that the Universe gives us what we want, just not always in the way we imagined.

Growing up with just my Mom, I always wanted the big family that I felt like everyone else had except for me. I will stand around tomorrow and watch everyone take family pictures as I stand to the side and ask someone to snap a picture of just myself and my Mom. I will walk down the stage and look out to only find one set of eyes staring back at me. Come Sunday, though, I will finally find my family, teams, and togetherness. When we take pictures, it will be in groups of teams. When I walk out from the side of the stage and look out into the audience, I will not see one set of eyes- I will see an audience full of people cheering together. One of the biggest reasons I've stayed involved in coaching for so long is for that culture of together. Walking into an arena wearing the same colors, for the same reason creates a feeling of belonging and home; and I can't wait to make that arena feel like the fresh start to a new home on Sunday.

SEASON ONE
SUNDAY, DECEMBER 16, 2007

Four months ago, we had just finally gotten into the gym. had no air, no power, and no lights.

We had nothing.

Time went by and all the problems got fixed. The electric and lights were finally turned on, along with the air conditioning. We had the basics and were able to start REALLY practicing and putting the routines together.

And now, four months later- here we are. Competing tomorrow at our first competition, in our first season, at our first showing to the world of what we can do. There was a time I was so worried that this day would never come. People told me I would never be able to open a gym at my age. It would be a joke. No one would come and I was just way too young to be able to handle coaching all the teams and running a business at the same time.

But sure enough, we had our registrations back in May and we got enough girls to have two senior aged teams. When I thought the gym would never be finished- it got finished (two months late, but it did get finished.) When I thought that the energy company would never come out and turn on our power- they did (two weeks late- but it did get done.) We might not have gotten exactly what we wanted at the exact time we wanted it- but it did work out.

I guess the moral of this story is that no matter what happens, everything will work itself out. Tomorrow is our first competition. First competition ever! No matter what happens tomorrow- you all are already a success. You have only been practicing together for four months. Look how far you have made it!!! We still have a long way to go, but I know we will get there- I know we will make it. If there is anyone in the world who can do what we have done- it's us. Take a step back and look at what you have accomplished this far.

Are there things we can improve upon for the future? Always.

But look how far you are right now. If you can do this in four months- just imagine what you could do by next year- or the next. Not just in cheerleading, but in life. You really can reach your goals and I hope the past four months have shown you to never, ever give up. No matter how bad it is or how bad it seems- it will work itself out.

I just started re-reading this from the top and I read the third sentence that I wrote.

"We had nothing."

That is completely wrong.

Because when I look back- we had everything. We had each other, and as cheesy as that sounds- that's all we needed. We just needed something to believe in. I believed in you all and that's what kept me going. When everything else seemed to be going wrong- I knew I had to keep going because I couldn't let you all down. I don't know what I would do without you guys. I am so, so grateful for your support and dedication. Thank you for believing. You all have given me so much and I don't think I will ever be able to truly explain how thankful I am for every single one of you. I know that each one of us was brought together for a reason. And that reason has nothing to do with cheerleading.

You girls inspire me to work harder and to never give up; you have all already taught me so much. Every day you walk in the door proves that nothing is impossible, truly nothing.

The competition this weekend is not the end- it is a beginning to a great season that is about to start. I hope you walk on stage with your head up and can be proud of how far you've already come. I know you are nervous. I know you are worried about your stunts hitting. But do you really think I would let you do those stunts at competition if I didn't believe that they would hit?

Practices can be rough. Especially lately, I know they are frustrating at times too. But don't give up, because the second you give up is the second you lose. No matter what, you've got to keep going, keep fighting, and keep believing. Sometimes things have to be believed before they are seen. You have to believe that you can do it or you will never be able to do it.

So today, tomorrow, and for the rest of this season I ask you to believe in yourselves, believe in each other, and believe in everything that this team can be.

Just believe.

SEASON ONE
SUNDAY, DECEMBER 16, 2007

I can't tell you how many people laughed in my face when I told them I was opening a cheerleading gym.

A cheerleading gym?
I can't tell you how many people thought I was crazy.

Is that even a real business?
People I trusted would tell me to my face how excited they were for me and then those same people went behind my back and told people that I had no idea what I was doing. People told me that no one would ever come and it would be impossible for someone my age to open a business- a gym for that matter. Deep down, I truly believed that if I opened a gym- people would come.

And you came.

For that, I truly want to thank you. Thank you for believing in me and thank you for believing in Shine. Thank you for taking a chance when no one else would. Thank you for sticking up for Shine when everyone doubted us. Thank you for sticking with it when times got hard. Thank you for practicing hard when you didn't want to. Thank you for believing.

Looking back at the past few months there were a lot of things that seemed impossible. It seemed impossible that the gym would ever get finished- with air, with lights and everything else. It seemed impossible that a group of girls could actually get along and be a successful team. It seemed impossible that we would ever learn a full routine with functioning parts.

But it's finally all falling into place. Finally, it all seems possible. Everything we have accomplished this far- there has been someone saying that it would be impossible.

But here's the thing, not just in cheerleading, but in life- there will always be people who want to bring you down. People who tell you what you cannot do. People who tell you that "it's not possible."

Don't ever listen to them. Don't ever let someone else define your version of possible.

I will never stop believing in you and I will never stop believing in everything that you are and that you can be. You can do this, but you have to start believing in yourselves. Put your head up and be proud of yourselves! I hope you walk into that competition on Sunday like you own the place. Find me another team that could do what you did in four months. I guarantee you there is no one out there that can do what you did. You have overcome so much and in such a little amount of time!!! Look at the big picture!

I am already so proud of you girls- I can't even explain how much you have done for me. You made my impossible become possible and there is nothing I can ever do to repay you all for that. I hope that if there is one thing you take away from cheering at Shine and one thing that I can give back to you, it is this:

"Nothing is impossible if you believe."

Really and truly- there is nothing you cannot do if you work hard enough. Never give up and never stop believing in the possibility of everything you can be. Because when you look back at the end of the day, that's what life is all about. It's the possibilities that keep us going... not the guarantees.

SEASON ONE
JANUARY 2008

"Never let anyone turn your sky into a ceiling."

- Unknown

I knocked down a wall today.

Literally, but I guess in a lot of other ways too.

We expanded the gym and leased the space next door.

It's surreal to think that a few months ago, I wasn't really sure if anyone would show up at all and now, we're breaking down walls to have a bigger gym.

When we distance ourselves from other people, or bigger dreams, or taking new chances we really just box ourselves in to mediocrity. The only real walls that can ever contain us are the ones we put ourselves in.

I guess that's the good thing about walls though, we can always tear them down.

SEASON ONE
FEBRUARY 2008

The little details are going to make this competition for you.

Have you been putting in the extra time that it's going to take to get one step ahead of everyone else?

You should be practicing extra every single night, in front of a mirror. Stretch, jump, tumble, go for a run… every extra effort you put in now is going to propel you forward. There is no one on this team who is perfect, everyone can improve on something.

If you are willing to put in the extra time and effort this week to improve it will pay off in a big way on Saturday.

Also, just a little something to think about—

A couple weeks ago there was this thing called the Super Bowl that a few billion people all over the world watched. If you didn't know, the New York Giants won the Super Bowl. However, the main point to keep in mind about this game is just how it started.

At the beginning of the season, the New York Giants lost. Not once, but twice. The Giants season started this year with zero wins and two losses.

Everyone had written them off, their coach was close to getting fired, and people were quickly beginning to doubt if they could turn their season around. After two losses, I'd imagine that even the team themselves wondered if they would get a win.

I can only imagine the locker room talk. Do you really think everyone stayed positive and was able to get along? Do you really think there were players who didn't want to give up?

I'm sure it was tough. But somehow, together, they realized that instead of dwelling on the mistakes and pointing fingers, they could rally together and work together as a team to turn it all around.

Everyone on the Giants, from coaches to players to equipment managers, worked together. Everyone worked hard to improve their skills and improve their dedication to the team. They dedicated themselves to working harder and showing their character and heart. The players put in hours upon hours of extra time to improve themselves for the team. When things got rough for them, they kept going. They lifted each other up and supported each other. They believed in each other and what they could do together.

They not only became a better team after their losses, they became the team that won the Super Bowl that year.

Think about it.
Third times a charm- don't let this chance pass you by.

Believe.

SEASON ONE
MARCH 2008

Stop doubting yourselves and start pushing yourselves.

We might not have had the season we had wanted.
We might not have won competitions that we should have.
But that's the past and this is now.

No one cares how you start... they care how you finish.
Finish it on top.

Remember, in the end- everything works out the way it is supposed to.

And this is how it's supposed to be.

Dream big and big things will happen.

SEASON ONE
APRIL 2008

"To believe... is to know that every day is a new beginning. It is to trust that miracles happen, and dreams really do come true.

To believe... is to see Angels dancing among the clouds, to know the wonder of a stardust sky, and the wisdom of the man in the moon.

To believe... is to find the strength and courage that lies within us. When it is time to pick up the pieces and begin again.

To believe... is to know we are not alone, that life is a gift and this is our time to cherish it.

To believe... is to know that wonderful surprises are just waiting to happen, and all our hopes and dreams are within reach. If only we believe."

- *C'est La Vi by Lancelot*

I have been waiting to give you this letter for a LONG time. I started writing it before our first competition and I added some more into it last night. I wanted to tell you why you are called team destiny. I have never told anyone why I chose that name for you, so here it goes.

When I was in high school, I signed up to volunteer coach a recreational youth cheerleading team. At first they told me that all the junior coaching positions were full and unfortunately, I wasn't going to be able to coach. However, a few weeks later I got a phone call letting me know that a spot had opened up and I would be able to junior coach a peewee aged cheerleading team. I was so excited and I gladly accepted.

Two of my friends were also junior coaching and I thought it would be a lot of fun. That first year was awesome. I really loved coaching and I was really excited to go back the next year and do it again. In fact, the next year I coached the same girls again in the next age bracket up and the year after, I progressed up with them again to the maximum age group in the program which was eighth grade. The year that I coached that team of eighth graders, I was a senior in high school and I was getting ready to go to college, so I knew that it would be the last time I ever coached.

I put everything I had into that group of girls and that final season meant so much to me because I knew it would be my last. The girls on that team were very special to me- as I had coached them all for three years and I just didn't think I could ever coach any other group of girls again and feel so attached to them.

At the year-end banquet I was approached by the coach of another team who asked if I would come and coach for her team next year. I said no. A month or so later she called me again. By this time I was going through cheerleading withdrawals. I missed it and although I knew it would be different girls- I accepted the job to coach. I ended up coaching another great group of kids, however- this team was very different, as they were already in their final season, all eighth graders, which made it a whole new challenge. It was a hard year and a learning experience getting used to a new group of kids who I was unfamiliar with.

Those girls were used to their old coaches that they had in the past and weren't used to me or my style of coaching. It was a really hard season and by the end of the it I decided (once again) I was done with coaching.

But it's pretty clear now that that's not where the story ends.

Fast forward to the next year, I was again asked to coach and again, I declined. I actually offered to come in and help out from time to time, but I just wasn't ready to commit back to coaching another team again.

A few days before the start of practices, my Mom got really sick. I had to spend all of my time with her, to help make sure she was okay. I completely forgot about cheerleading and all of my priorities were on helping my Mom.

After a week or two, it was my Mom who encouraged me to take a break and go check out the cheerleading team that I had semi committed to helping. After debating if I should even go at all, I went.

I felt like a beginner again. A new start or maybe it was just an escape from everything else that was going on. What started out as me helping out from time to time became my full time love and greatest passion. It is that team that made me fall in love with cheerleading all over again.

The rest, is history.

The year I thought that cheerleading was over with for good was the year I decided to start a gym. The next year I coached those same girls again- and planned on and worked on Shine for the whole year.

No one really knew anything about Shine and most people didn't really believe it was going to happen. And it was not something that happened overnight.

It took a lot of planning and there were times that I wanted to give up.

The first time I went and applied for a loan- I got denied.

The first time I found a building that I was in love with- the perfect size the perfect place- it was in the wrong zoning district and I was told I couldn't put a gym there.

The first time I handed out flyers for shine- no one took any.

I know this is a long story- but I guess what I'm trying to tell you is that everything we do and everything that happens to us- is supposed to happen to us. It's our destiny. We can't always tell at the time where the road is leading, but we have to believe it's leading us the right way. I can't tell you how many nights that I cried because I thought this moment would never happen. I can't tell you how many times I watched college nationals on tape and dreamed of one day coaching a team that would get to perform on the Bandshell stage in Daytona Beach. And I can't tell you how grateful I am to you for being on this team.

Whether we realize it or not, the things that have happened to us in the past- those things happen to us to guide us along the right path to where we are supposed to be in our future. If I had never gotten offered to be a coach, if I had never gone back to coach that team, or if I had stopped looking for a gym and given up..... Who knows what would have happened. But here we are. April 12th, 2008 standing outside next to Daytona Beach, and that is what destiny is all about.

It's about realizing that at this very moment- this is exactly where you are meant to be. Right here, right now you are meant to be reading this letter. And you are meant to be on this team. Everything that has happened to this team is for a reason. Every struggle and every discouragement- although we may not understand it- this is how the season was meant to be. We must believe that.

And deep down inside of you- no matter how discouraged you might feel- I know that deep down inside of you is that belief: the belief that you CAN hit everything in your routine today, that you CAN perform better than everyone else today, and that you CAN win today.

I know it's still there because each and every one of you had that belief inside of you at the beginning of this season. The season hasn't been perfect- but it has been ours, together, with every struggle along the way. Sometimes, struggles are exactly what we need in our life. If we were to go through our life without any obstacles, we would be crippled. We would not be as strong as what we could have been. Give every opportunity a chance, leave no room for regrets.

That is all I am hoping for you all today. I just want you to believe in yourselves, give it one more chance, and give your all one more time. You will never again dance to this same music or perform this same routine. For some of you- you will never again get to compete on a stage right next to the beach, with the open sky above you. When you run onto the stage to perform today, look up. It's a big world under a big sky and no one knows exactly where the future will lead, but I know for sure that each and every one of you will go forward to do fabulous things. More importantly, when you look up at the sky, think about right now; because right now you are meant to be on that stage and you are meant to perform today on this team. And today when you perform, do it for the struggle.

Do it for every single person who told you that you couldn't.

Do it because it's your destiny.

SEASON ONE
APRIL 2008

Have you ever wondered why you are named team infinity? Ever wonder why I gave you that name? Well here you go- this letter should explain why you are named team infinity.

Infinity is defined as unboundedness. It refers to several distinct concepts usually linked to the idea of "without end" or "bigger than the biggest thing you can think of." In the dictionary infinity means "no limits" and Infinity is commonly known by the sideways figure eight symbol.

I wanted to name you team infinity because I never wanted there to be a limit on you. I wanted you to push yourselves as hard as you could and go as far as you could this season. I guess if there is one thing I want you to get out of cheering at Shine- it is that you can do anything. You have no limits- and if you put your mind to something, you really can do it. Just believe in all of the possibilities that are out there waiting for you. Remember- life is about the possibilities- not the guarantees.

You'll never get to dance to this music again and you will never get to walk out on that stage and compete here again.
This is it.

All season it has seemed like we have had limits. Right when we think we have it- we get stopped. We reach the limit and we just stop.
Today-- this moment, this competition, this beach represents our limits. Today is the day that we forget our limits and throw them away. Today is the day we stop listening to what other

people think about us and make up our minds what we think of ourselves. Do you think you are talented? Do you think this is a good team? Do you think you can win this competition today? I think so and I know that deep down inside of you- you think it too. It may be hard with all the limits we have encountered this season- but deep down I know you think you are the best. And that is all that really matters. Think it- be it- make it come true.

Today is the day that you prove that we are team infinity. You have no limits. You can do this.

Look in front of you. No really- look up- Look up in front of you right now. The world is yours. Look around you. Look next to you.

You may not realize it yet- but everything you need you already have. Everything you need is already inside of you. The things ahead of you will be more amazing than you ever could imagine. The world is out there waiting for you and waiting to see all of the amazing things you can do. And today is only a very small part of that.

Years from now, when you are grown up and successful, at the grocery store- or at the mall- or out to dinner with friends and you see it, the figure out infinity symbol, I hope you think of Shine. I hope you think of this team. But most importantly I hope you think of this moment. I hope you think of this moment on the beach with team infinity.

Because right here, right now- this moment is perfect and I couldn't picture it any other way with any other girls or any other team. And this moment right here, right now is a memory that no one can ever take away from us and it is a memory that no one else would ever understand. This moment represents the moment that you decided to throw away your limits and GO FOR IT.

Although this team will never be together again- we will always have this moment together. We will always have our memories of how this story began together, and in our memories, we can take this moment- here on this beach, together- and we can make it last forever.

This moment is infinity.

"Take a minute and try to answer the following questions:

1. Name the five wealthiest people in the world.
2. Name the last five Heisman trophy winners.
3. Name the last five winners of the Miss USA pageant.
4. Name ten people who have won the Nobel Prize.
5. Name the last decade's worth of World Series winners.

How did you do?
None of us remember the headliners of yesterday.
The applause dies. Awards tarnish. Achievements are forgotten. Accolades and certificates are buried with their owners.

1. List a teacher who aided your journey through school.
2. Name a friend who helped you through a tough time.
3. Name someone who taught you something worthwhile.
4. Think of someone who makes you feel appreciated.
5. Think of three people you enjoy spending time with.

Easier?
Always remember, the people who make a difference in your life are not the ones with the most credentials, the most money, or the most awards. They are the ones that care."

-Attributed to Dennis Fakes

SEASON 2 LETTERS

"If you believe it will work out...you'll see opportunities.
If you believe it won't... you'll see obstacles."
                                        -Wayne Dyer

SEASON TWO
DECEMBER 4, 2008

On Sunday I videotaped your routine from the opening stunt to the end. I started the music and ran into the parent viewing area with the video camera trying to get back there in time to video tape the stunt and the rest of the entire routine. As I was standing there taping and watching, there were two moms sitting down whispering next to me. Both of the Moms' daughters cheer for their youth Recreational Cheerleading team and they just take tumble classes at Shine. One of the mom's daughters is a regular in the one o'clock tumble class so she is always there while you all have your practice. The other mom had brought her daughter to try a tumble class and had never been to Shine before.

I overheard one Mom ask the other Mom how Shine cheerleading was different from her daughter's recreational cheerleading league. The Mom explained that rec cheerleading teams cheer for a football team and then do competition, whereas all-star cheerleading only does competitions. After she said that she went on to tell the other mom to hush and that she needed to "watch this, watch this."

As you did your tumbling section- I was trying to pay attention to who was on count, who wasn't throwing their pass, who wasn't transitioning cleanly- but I kept getting distracted by the first mom telling the other mom "watch this," "look at them tumble," "they are just amazing!"

"Can you believe they can do all that? Look at that," and then as you moved into jumps, "Look at their jumps, they do three jumps!?!" And as you moved into the double downs "Wow that looks cool!"

"These kids are amazing!"

"Oh watch this, they spin up and down," and as I was trying to keep track of who was off count, who didn't double down, and who wasn't transitioning, the moms just kept going.

"Yeah, this is their cheer, their routine is to music, it's so cool," as you moved to baskets, "Oh watch this- look how high they go in the air" (kick fulls go) "WOW!!!"

As the pyramid started they actually sat in silence and then as you hit your pyramid the mom said, "Wow, these kids must have been doing this forever" and then – as you were transitioning to the dance - the new mom asked the other mom "How long do you think they have been doing this?" The other mom said, "Shhhhh- and tapped her on the leg- WATCH THIS, WATCH THIS (her eyes on you all the whole time) she said "This is the best part, this is the best part watch this!" And then you did your dance.

By the time the routine was over, I had lost track of the mistakes. I wasn't focused any longer on the momentary errors; these two Moms had made me see the bigger picture.

Sometimes, I think the best thing we can do (and I can do- as a coach) is to take a step back and look at how far you have come and how much you have accomplished. Are you done? No. Do you still need to work hard? Yes. Are there things we can all do better? Yes. But at the end of the day, no matter how much yelling, or nit picking, or nagging that I do to you all- I really am amazed by your talent, endurance and hard work.

I am so proud of you and I believe in you and this team.

I close my eyes and see the perfect routine.

I close my eyes and see the entire pyramid in the air and the crowd cheering along to the beat of the music.

I close my eyes and I see the looks of joy on your faces that will come when you hit your entire routine. I know you can do it.

I believe that you can do it.

The real moment of success is not the moment that is obvious to the crowd; and it is days like today that teach us the importance of the journey.

SEASON TWO
DECEMBER 31, 2008
E-MAIL TO: ALL

As 2008 comes to an end, it is time for us to look back at what the year has brought us. Our second season, the 2008-2009 Cheer Season began in May and brought us many new athletes and many returnees. The summer months were long and hard practices for the girls but they stuck through it to make it to the competition season.

Last season, our tiny team was exhibition only. This year we decided to compete them against other teams in their age group. This team, made up of 4 and 5 year olds, took home 1st place at the Central Florida Championships in Lakeland. What a big accomplishment for our tiny athletes!

Our Youth team has worked hard on their tumbling and stunting skills over the summer and was able to move up to level 2. Their first competition was the Central Florida Open Championship and they took home 3rd place out of 4 teams. Our youth team was a small team and had to compete against large youth teams at this competition, but they were able to hold their own. With the addition of new athletes to the youth team from half season sign- ups our youth team will now be competing in the large division for the rest of the season!

We now also have another Junior aged team that will be our half season team. They will start competing in March and we are looking forward to a great season with our new half season girls!

Our Senior one team took home 1st place at their first competition of the season and then 1st place also at the Central

Florida Championships. What a big accomplishment for these girls! All of the girls on this team came brand new to Shine this season and had never done competitive cheer before. I am so impressed with their drive and hard work to make themselves better. We are hoping this team will remain undefeated all season long. We want to continue to add more difficulty into this routine to make sure their routine is untouchable by the competition!

Our Senior two team took home 3rd place at their first competition of the year and then went on to take home 2nd place out of 6 teams at the Central Florida Championships! In fact, they even beat the teams they competed against during their first competition- proving what we had known all along- that they are a big contender in their division. When you watch this group of girls perform, it is hard to take your eyes off of them. We are going to continue to work on timing and add more tumbling and difficulty into the routine. I know the girls are hungry for a first place win and I have no doubt that it will be coming their way soon.

Our Senior four team took home 3rd place at their first event and then 1st place at the Central Florida Championships. They also won the grand championship level 4 award, meaning that out of all the level 4 teams (large, small, coed) they had the highest score. This was a big accomplishment for the girls and very well deserved. This team has set many goals for themselves this season and will continue to improve as the season progresses.

At the Central Florida Championships, there was a lot to be proud of! We received zero deductions all day. We took home 3 first places, 1 second place, and 1 third place. But most importantly our girls had the best behavior and sportsmanship. All day I heard nothing but good things from other people, coaches, and parents. We can't control what other teams do and say, but we can control our actions. I am so happy with the girls for cheering on other teams and wishing others good luck.

Also, thank you so much to all of the parents who came down to the front rows to cheer our teams on while they performed. It makes such a big difference when we have a big crowd cheering the teams on!

I am so proud of all of our team's accomplishments so far this season. But more importantly I am so proud to look back at these girls and think about how far they have come. So many girls have learned new skills, new stunts, new tumbling, and are doing things that they once thought they never could.

Two years ago at this time, we had no gym. Shine Athletics was a vision in my head, something I dreamed that would one day come true. As I sit here and mail out this letter to the 100+ families that are now a part of Shine Athletics I am overwhelmed with gratitude to each and every one of you. I believe that this is still only the beginning of something much bigger than I ever hoped for and I believe that 2009 will be an unforgettable year for us all.

Thank you for your support and thank you for continuing to believe in the endless possibilities of what we can do!

Happy New Year!

SEASON TWO
FEBRUARY 2009

"Winners compare their achievements with their goals, while losers compare their achievements with those of other people."

-Nido Qubein

As we go into competition this weekend, let's focus on our goals and our dreams.

Our goal is to hit the routine. If we can do that, then we have met out first goal of the season.

I believe in each and every one of you with all of my heart. I know that you have the talent, drive, and ability to perform that routine like it needs to be performed.

For those two minutes I want to see the dedication, the desire, and the drive in your eyes.

If you want it, it's yours.

Go get it.
And most importantly, believe.

SEASON TWO
APRIL 2009

"Sometimes, struggles are exactly what we need in our life. If we were to go through our life without any obstacles, we would be crippled. We would not be as strong as what we could have been. Give every opportunity a chance, leave no room for regrets."

-Anonymous

I've thought all week about what to say to you all right now. I close my eyes and I see you on that stage. I close my eyes and I can picture it already. I see it. I want a win for you so bad.

Every time I sit down to write this letter I flashback. From the summer, the practices- the routines, all the obstacles you have overcome, all the excitement, all the joy, all the heartbreak, and all the time it has taken you to get here. I close my eyes and I see each and every one of your faces, your smiles, your attitudes, your laughs. I close my eyes and I see the sadness and the disappointment too. I close my eyes and I see the stage you will perform on, next to the ocean, and I hear them calling out the placements. I can hear it. I hear your name. I want this to be yours today.

Sometimes, it takes many tries to get something right and I believe that today is your day to get it right.

It took Macy's seven tried to become an actual store and take off.
Henry Ford's first two auto businesses failed. I guess third time was a charm.

Michael Jordan didn't make it the first time he tried out for his high school basketball team
Babe Ruth struck out 1,330 times.

These statistics are proof that it's easy to count the failures. But they also prove that failure doesn't last.

No one sees any of those people or stores as failures, even though they have failed before. They are successful because they kept trying.

It's not always easy to hold your head up and give it another shot.
But that's what I'm begging you to do today.

I know it's not always easy. But today, please don't worry about failure. Worry about the chance you might miss today if you don't give it your all.
I'm telling you right now- it's going to be close. But I know you can do it.

It's not even a question of IF you can do it.
Everybody out there- including you- knows you can do it.
It's a question of WILL you do it.

Don't live down to other people's expectations- go out there today and be the game changer! Do it! I know you can!

Stay positive. Stay you. Keep believing and don't ever give up.
I know you believe it. And I know that belief is still inside of you.

The belief that you can hit everything in your routine today.

The belief that you can perform better than everyone else today.

The belief that you are the best team today.
And the belief that you can win today.

I know it's still there because each one of you had that inside of you at the beginning of this season. This season hasn't been perfect- but it has been ours, together- with every struggle along the way.

I know that deep down you know you can do it today. I just want you to believe in yourselves. Please just give it one more chance and give it all you've got one more time. Today I want you to perform like it was impossible to fail.

It's time to change the game! And it's up to you.

The time is now. STOP questioning yourself, stop doubting yourself and BE CONFIDENT!

What's stopping you?

SEASON TWO
APRIL 2009

"The few who do are the envy of the many who only watch."

-Jim Rohn

For every team, no matter how great they are- there is always something they can improve upon. For that reason I don't believe in perfect cheerleading routines. However, I do believe in perfect moments.

Every time I stand back stage with you, it's hard for me to walk away. I look at you all- behind the curtain, behind the stage, before you are about to perform- and it's hard. I just want to bottle that moment up and keep it in a jar forever. Because in that moment, before you compete, is all of your excitement, your hope, and your vision for hitting a routine that you know can give you the win that you want.

Today, when you run out onto the stage and I am standing nearby- as your biggest fan- I'm going to have that moment of hope to hold onto and a moment of memories to reflect upon. As you take the stage and walk onto the floor, I'll think about the grueling summer practices. How all of you attempted to be better than you ever thought you could be, the moments of cheering on your teammates, and the moments of disappointment that you've experienced. All the excitement, the highs, the lows, the happiness, the heartbreak, and all the time it has taken each one of you to get to here. Back again to hope. Back again to one more chance. Back again to give it all you've got.

Success is not a destination- it's a journey and this season has truly defined that quote. It has been our journey together.

Today you have an opportunity to go out on that stage and show everyone what cheerleading is all about. It's about being a TEAM. You get to be the teacher today. You can teach a lesson today to everyone who is watching you. You are redefining what success should really be defined as. It's not first place that matters most today- it's the fact that through everything- through all the ups and downs, you never turned your backs on each other. That's what a team is. That's what cheerleading is. It's believing in each and every team mate next to you. It's putting emotion into your performance. It's proving to everyone watching that you want it the most. More than other teams can even imagine.

Today, I get to be YOUR biggest cheerleader. My favorite moments aren't coaching or correcting you, my favorite moments are when I get to be your biggest fan. Watching the hard work unfold onstage is the greatest gift for me.

So today, before your actual performance, I will cherish the moments of hope and reflection before the real show even starts.

And as you walk on stage, in those last moments, I already know what I will see.

I will see the team that believes in their stunts- even though they have fallen before.

I will see the team who believes in the tumblers- even though they have busted before.

I will see 20 girls who believe in each other and believe in their team- even though they've lost before.

I will see the definition of a team. A team ready to look the world straight in the eye. Not just ready, but smiling. Smiling because they know they are prepared.

And in that moment, before it all begins- the moment that I can instantly see the entire season that has led to this moment play out in my head - I will see *perfection.*

And then the music will play.

I love you all.

Thank you for making me a better person.
You are my inspiration.
You are my perfection.

"Now is the time to look ahead into our future.
We can accomplish anything we set our minds to.
We have proved to ourselves, that we are no longer lost;
that we have found a path to lead us into greater things."
- Unknown

SEASON 3 LETTERS

"Begin doing now what you want to do.
We are not living in an eternity, we only have this
moment, sparkling like a star in our hand and
melting like a snowflake."
                                        -Francis Bacon

SEASON THREE
JUNE 2009
E-MAIL TO: ALL

Dear Shine Families,

As I am sure everyone has heard the news about the Wood
Family, I wanted to make sure everyone knew about the
Remembrance being held tomorrow evening. All friends and
family are asked to attend and bring a candle.

The Candlelight Remembrance for the Wood Family will take
place at 7:30pm and is being held at the Heathrow Pool outside.

Aubrey cheered at Shine Athletics for two years on our half
season team. Her family had been a part of Shine Athletics since
our first season open.

As a program, we are devastated by her loss. She was a happy,
bubbly child and will be greatly missed by all of us. She will
always be a part of our family at Shine Athletics and it is my
hope that Shine Athletics cheerleaders will attend tomorrow
evening to remember her and her family. We will be closing the
gym tomorrow at 7pm to leave and go the remembrance for the
family.

We will be meeting at Shine Athletics at 7pm and carpooling
over together. Anyone is welcome to attend the remembrance
and meet at Heathrow Pool at 7:30 pm- or if you would like to
meet us at Shine Athletics at 7pm and carpool with us.

All Level 4 athletes- instead of practice please meet at the gym at

7pm so we can go over together. Teams who normally have practice from 6-7:30 will be ending early at 7pm so we can go to the remembrance.

Thank you,
Sydney

SEASON THREE
NOVEMBER 2009

There are certain things you don't get over.
There are certain phone calls you never forget.

I can't imagine losing a child as a parent.
I assume it's like drowning in darkness; a pool of grief that you can only rescue yourself from by clinging onto the tiny cracks of light that come from the happy memories of the past.

I don't know what it's like to lose a child as a parent. I pray that I never do. But I know what it's like to lose a child as a coach and the heartbreak that comes with it feels like the entire weight of the Earth just came crashing down onto your shoulders.

I remember standing in my bedroom and answering the phone call that told me the bad news.
It wasn't a flood of tears, it was an overwhelming disbelief. Shock. Hope that the news was wrong.

Once it settles in, your mind wanders back to the last practice. The last phone call, the last time…

I'm a fixer by nature. When someone's upset, I strive to make them feel better as quick as I can. When someone's hurt, I try to find the quickest way they can heal.
But how do you deal with something you can't fix?

When I first started coaching, I never thought I could love a team and group of kids as much as that very first team I ever worked with. I was in high school, a sophomore and a junior coach volunteer for a recreational youth cheerleading league that went up to 8th grade. The organization was created to serve as a feeder program for the local high school cheerleading and football programs- the athletes were zoned to teams based on their high school district and the athletes aged out after 8th grade to encourage the athletes to join their high school sports teams. I never saw myself coaching after high school, so I was pretty sure I had found the perfect scenario. Each year as the kids would move up an age bracket, I would move up a year in a high school. My senior year would be this group of athlete's 8th grade year of youth sports. We could go out on top together.

That group of kids taught me to not only love coaching, but love in general- and I am forever grateful for them. However, it is the group I coached after them- my freshman year of college- that taught me that love never divides. Love multiples.

I was so worried coaching different kids would take away from that first team, but I couldn't have been more wrong. It's like having multiple children, you don't love them less- you love them so much more.

Each and every athlete I have ever coached has expanded my heart and holds a piece of it with them.

That piece doesn't change if we have a winning season or a losing season, it holds strong because of the bond we created as a coach and athlete.

That piece also doesn't go away because of death. The tears I have are full of memories that will shine with love forever.

After the initial shock, I tried to fix things. I instantly set my sights on soothing the athletes that were friends with her.

What could we do to help? Could we organize something that could help ease the pain for these kids?

Her favorite color was yellow. She loved peace signs, and daisies, butterflies and brightness.

I went out and got heavy yellow foam papers that the kids could decorate for her.

They made them beautifully, with bright colors and her name. They were vibrant and light, like her.

It was expression for the other kids, for them it was healing through art.

They put them on her grave for her with yellow balloons.

It really was beautiful in every way.

It wasn't until much later that I really processed everything.

I still don't think I have fully processed everything and I'm not sure if I ever will.

I wanted to write something beautiful, that explained how I felt.

But I haven't figured that out yet.

There are still really dark moments. Moments where I just don't understand why a child is gone. Moments where I just don't understand how this could happen.

I try to teach that things happen for a reason, to trust fate, to trust God, and to always believe.

And this, this I just don't want to believe.

I try to relive the last times over and over.

Did I tell her to stop talking at the last practice I saw her at?

Did I coach her too hard?

Did she have fun?

Did she leave happy?

Did I ever tell her what a great kid she was?

Did I do as much as I could for her, while I still had the chance?

I prayed for a sign and I prayed for what to do for a long time.

I am trying to help the memory live on; I am trying to see the light in the darkness.

I was walking this morning, in a hurry, paying no attention to anyone but myself- and a little flutter caught my eye.
It was a yellow butterfly. Pale yellow, low flying, almost just asking to be seen. And in that moment, I knew.

There are days for healing and there are days for hurting.

But everyday there is love; the love never decreases, divides, or fades.

Love grows, love multiplies, and love shines on.

SEASON THREE
DECEMBER 2009
EVENT PROGRAM BOOK

Welcome to the Full Circle Showcase!

Our goal is to make this an annual event with even more teams in the following years. We want to promote positive sportsmanship and camaraderie between multiple cheerleading organizations and teams. The competition season flies by so quickly, the Showcase is a great way for our athletes to get some extra time to show off their skills.

All proceeds from today's event will go to the Aubrey Wood Memorial Scholarship Fund. This fund is set up through the Shine Athletics nonprofit booster club. The scholarship will be open to cheerleaders in the Central Florida area who are in need of registration, competition, or uniform fees- whether it be for an all-star cheer program, rec program, or school program. More information on how to apply for the fund will be available through the Shine Athletics website.

This event personally is a HUGE deal to all of us at Shine Athletics, especially me. It's more than just cheerleading. It's about coming together, supporting the sport, and giving back. I am so thankful to everyone who has helped me and the kids at Shine Athletics over the past two and a half years. I can positively say, that without the support of an amazing group of people- we would not be having this event today.

A huge thank you is in order to everyone who has helped make this event possible. All of the Shine Athletics parents who have volunteered their time and energy into this event. All of the volunteers working the tables today and the volunteers who set up our spring floor. Thank you to Lake Mary High School for hold our event as well. And thank YOU, for coming out and being a part of the first annual Full Circle Showcase.

I couldn't pick a better group of kids or a better community to get to work with. And I couldn't pick a better group of teams to perform today. Two and a half years ago, an event like this would have seemed impossible.

Today, I stand here with the belief that dreams do come true and together, we can make a difference.

SEASON THREE
DECEMBER 2009

As we go to competition this Saturday, we need to focus on your first goal of the season- execution.

I believe in each and every one of you. I know you all have the ability to perform this routine and hit this routine. But you have to be able to do that AS a team.

When we blame each other for our mistakes and point the finger at someone who isn't getting their job done- it separates the team. This is YOUR team. And if someone is having trouble with a skill, instead of blaming them- why don't you ask them how you can help them? It's not about you. It's not about your stunt. It's not about your tumbling pass. It's about your team as a whole.

If your tumbling pass isn't landing- why aren't you coming into the gym every day this week to work on it? If your stunt isn't hitting, why don't you ask your stunt group to come in an extra day and work on it? You can't be successful when you blame others and don't do anything to help them. You have to give it your all and you have to reach out and help others on your team as well.

You rise by lifting others. When you stop focusing on YOU and put the focus on YOUR TEAM- that is when you will truly become successful as a team.

It doesn't matter what happened in the past, at practice, or at the last competition. You can sit around and point fingers at other people, or you can get up and work harder. You have the choice and opportunity to make this weekend turn out in your favor.

As a coach, your goal has been met not by placement but by performance and execution. If you hit your routine you can walk away knowing that you did the best you can do, you will never have to look back and wonder if the results would have been different based on a different performance. This Saturday- it's really not about winning. It's about hitting the routine and executing the routine AS A TEAM.

Over the summer, I loved watching you practice. Why? Because every practice- you pushed each other, you clapped for each other, you encouraged each other. You were a team.

But now, when I go to practice, I don't see a team. I see 19 girls at cheer practice. You complain about each other and say- I didn't hit my stunt because of her, or I didn't tumble because she was in my way, or I can't do this, or did you see her? She messed up. Well, in case you forgot- SHE is on YOUR team. Don't turn your backs on someone because they are struggling. Reach out and help them.

If you go back to caring about the TEAM, this weekend you will do much better than caring about just yourself.

You can make excuses or you can make it happen. Refuse to give up.

SEASON THREE
JANUARY 2010

Discouraged? The following story is one of my favorites:

As I was driving home from work one day, I stopped to watch a local little League baseball game that was being played in a park near my home. As I sat down behind the bench on the first-baseline, I asked one of the boys what the score was.

"We're behind 14 to nothing," he answered with a smile.
"Really," I said. "I have to say you don't look very discouraged."

"Discouraged?" the boy asked with a puzzled look on his face.
"Why should we be discouraged? We haven't been up to bat yet."

Don't give up before you play the game.
Never give up

Abraham Lincoln said, "People are just about as successful as they make up their minds to be."
And he's right.
If you want to be successful, then be it. No one can stop you from being successful this weekend, except you.

SEASON THREE
FEBRUARY 2010

What if I told you, you couldn't lose.

What if I told you that the people in charge of the competition called me and offered us an automatic fifth place to ensure that we would come back again next year. They said we want to guarantee your business with us, so we want to give your team an automatic fifth place in their division. 5th place out of 9 teams sounds like a pretty good guarantee.

You would still do your routine and compete. But you would automatically get fifth place. You could drop or hit- it wouldn't matter. Just an automatic deal to get fifth place.

Deal or no deal? Would you take it? Would you settle for fifth place to guarantee that you wouldn't lose?

I recently heard a story that is now one of my favorites of all time.

A professor stood in front of his class on final exam day. As he passed out the exams he told his students that he understood the pressure they were under and he knew for many of them, they just needed a passing grade to move on and out of his class.

He told the class that he would offer an automatic B grade to any student who would like to forego taking the Final exam and leave.

Over half of the class cheered, thanked the professor, and left. Only seven students remained.

The professor asked one last time if there was anyone else who wanted to leave before the exam started.

One more student left.

He was down to six.

The professor then closed the door to the exam room, took attendance, and handed out the final exam.

There were two sentences typed on the paper:

'Congratulations, you have just received an 'A' in this class. Keep believing in yourself.'

The students who didn't believe that they could ace the exam or get an A on the exam are the students that left. Any student or athlete that doesn't have the confidence to ace the test or win the competition will only ever be a 'B' at best.

'A' students and athletes are those who believe in what they're doing and aren't afraid of a challenge.

Believing in yourself comes from knowing what you are really capable of doing. You might not win every time and you might not ace the test every time, but you'll never have the chance to win it all if you don't give it a try.

Success is only guaranteed in hindsight.

No one, not even the most successful people imaginable knew that they were going to be successful in the beginning. They just put one foot in front of the other and kept moving forward.

Don't doubt determination, it plays one of the largest factors in success. Stay focused and know that trying means you're never losing.

And when it comes to this weekend's competition…

You're not going to lose. And not because of a deal.

We all know what you are capable of this weekend.
Don't give up.
Don't settle.
Don't stop

The game is changing. Now is the time for you to Shine.

Life is about the possibilities. *Not* **the guarantees.**

(PS- if any of you actually would have said yes to 5th place I would be very upset. If there is one thing I want to teach you and one thing that you get out of shine- it's to never give up. Never, ever stop fighting for what you want)

SEASON THREE
FEBRUARY 2010
Faith and Fear

"Fear and faith may seem like opposites, but they have something in common. Both ask us to believe something we cannot see.

Fear says to believe the negative. Faith says to believe the positive.
Fear says 'You've been through so much, you'll never be happy.'
Faith says 'Your best days are coming soon- they are right in front of you.'

Fear will try to dominate your thoughts. If you allow it, fear will keep you awake at night. Fear will steal your joy, steal your enthusiasm. Fear will follow you like a dark cloud. Why live in fear? It takes just as much energy to worry as it does to be positive and believe. If you let God deal with your fears and just put faith that the situation will turn around and be to your advantage."

- Joel Osteen

It would be easy to look at the schedule for next weekend and be afraid. Every team in the division is a strong, good team. Every team though. Including us. Don't use your energy to worry- use your energy to believe. You may have a lot coming against you, but if you choose to ignore the negative, the negative can't get to you.

Fear says "You'll never beat them."
Faith says "All things are possible, when you believe."

For a long time I let the negative get to me. Not all the way, but it really bothered me. Whenever we went to certain competitions with certain gyms- I hated being there. They intimidated me. The things they said about me, about Shine, about us. It hurt. And I thought it would never get better. I used to spend hours on the internet trying to look up the teams we would go against to see if we had a chance. I was going about it all the wrong way. I was giving in to being afraid.

Next weekend we will no longer be afraid. We will not be intimidated by anyone. You have worked for your spot in that division and your name belongs to be there. You have worked just as hard, if not harder. You have practiced just as much, if not more.

It's time to stop doubting and start believing. Stop being negative. Just try it for one week. Every time you think something could go wrong, just turn it around and tell yourself it will go right.
No more fear. Confidence.
No more questions. Make your performance the answer.

Every word, every count, and every motion should be filled with emotion. Put on a show and let's make it our job to redefine success. Walk off that stage with the satisfaction that you truly did the most you could do. Make everyone remember your two minutes and thirty seconds.

There's a very famous story about a boy named David who has to battle with a giant named Goliath.

Goliath was triple David's size. Everyone tried to talk David out of facing the giant. They told him to give up, they told him it was hopeless. I mean, why take the chance if you already know you're going to lose?
But David knew differently. He believed that he not only had a chance, but he believed he could defeat any obstacle standing in his way.

When others told him that Goliath was too big to hit, David

didn't get mad, he simply replied and told them that he was too big to miss.

Big dreams and goals aren't too big to accomplish, they are too big to miss out on.

Many of the things we want are things we have to believe we can have, before we actually get them.

It is the people that breathe life into their dreams and stay positive who reach their goals and end up turning the things that they talk about into their reality.

The people who continually talk about having bad luck or tell the world that nothing good can happen to them, are actually just creating their own negative reality.

The words you speak, the thoughts you think, and the beliefs that you hold really do play a part in your life.

Believe that now is your time and believe that you already have everything you need to be successful.

Remember, it's always darkest right before the dawn.

SEASON THREE
FEBRUARY 2010
Together we believe

I remember the State Fair competition last year like it was yesterday. I remember it being so cold during warm ups and the wind blowing. I remember bringing our huge half season team to compete for their first competition and all of their little faces were so excited.

I remember the day, but it kind of all blurs together- when you're running back in forth from warm ups, from one performance to another- over and over again throughout the day- it all just kind of meshes together. I can't tell you exactly what place every team got last year. I can't tell you all the little details that went on during the day.

But my most vivid memory is of Aubrey. I remember she was so sick. So sick, her mom didn't want her to compete. But I convinced her mom it would only be two and a half minutes, she could do it. So they came. And the whole day she was sitting around, not really feeling very well. But as soon as it came time to perform, she was ready. She walked on the floor and everything worked out. She hit every stunt, she smiled the whole time, she truly performed- everything a coach could want out of a cheerleader to do during a routine- she did it. And she did it sick. For me. For her team. For you. For Shine. And the second it was over, her parents grabbed her and took her to an urgent care as her fever had gotten worse. They cared so much about her and they were so worried, standing right there on the side waiting for her to be done.

Success comes from the heart and Aubrey proved that last

year at Tampa State Fair. She would never let her team down by not getting her job done. She did everything in her power to make sure she could help her team along the way.

As coaches, that's all we ask from you. Do more than just go through the motions. Give it your all and leave your heart on the floor. It's a chance you have that you'll never get back.

Aubrey won't be out their cheering today, but I promise she will definitely be cheering you on.

There are so many people today that believe in you. So many people that want just want to see you do what you love. It's time to show the world what Shine is all about. It's about performing, it's about meaning, and it comes from the heart. It's not always about a first place trophy. It's about becoming something that people told us we could never be.

They said it was impossible. They said it would never happen. It's not and it did.

Today, you can do more than just walk through the motions on a stage. You can give back; you can give your best.
Remember- when you give the world the best you have. The best comes back to you.

Today is not about being on a certain level or a certain team. It's about wearing the name Shine across your chest. We are all one. When one team in the gym messes up, we all mess up. When one team in the gym hits their routine, we all hit our routine. It's time to appreciate each team as their own and be grateful for what we have together.

Coming together is connecting all of the puzzle pieces.

"You can make an audience see whatever you want them to see- if you yourself believe in it."

-Unknown

If you want people to believe in you, you also have to believe in them. Understand that your teammates around you deserve your support.

"Without faith in yourself and others, success is impossible."

-Harvey Mackay

One step at a time, you have the opportunity to lay the foundation for those athletes who come after you.

It's time to show that we are not separate teams and separate levels, we are Shine Athletics.

And together we believe.

SEASON THREE
MARCH 19, 2010

"The most common way people give up their power is by thinking they don't have any."

- Alice Walker

You can choose right here, right now to be a victim. Or you can choose to be a fighter.

You can choose to worry about your stunt, or you can choose to hit your stunt.

You can choose to worry about your tumbling, or you can choose to land your tumbling.

You can choose to wonder how the other teams did or you can choose to just focus on yours.

You can choose to look around nervously or walk onto the floor with confidence.

You can choose to just go through the motions or you can choose to be a performer.

Life is what we make it, always has been, always will be.

If you aren't going to do this thing 110%, with a smile and push yourself harder than you ever have before... Why are you even here today?

It may seem that your future and your performance today depends on many other things; but really, it depends on you.

Throughout the season you have faced disappointments and you haven't always gotten exactly what you wanted at competitions.

But it's your choice how you react to that. You can choose to carry that in to today and to be a victim who is nervous and scared. Or you can be a fighter and go all out ...

Do you want to be a piece in the game? Or do you want to be the person who creates the rules on how the game is played?

Remember.... Without pressure and without difficulty- you would never have a diamond.

You have to be willing to go after what you want. You have to be willing to create something new and try something you've never done before. Even if you're on the right track, you'll get run over if you just sit there!

From the minute you step on the floor, you have a job to do and it's your job to get it done.
It's far from over.

OBISTYD
Our belief is stronger than your doubt

SEASON THREE
MARCH 20, 2010

There are moments when life stops. Or maybe, moments when life stops you.

Kids get hurt. It's the nature of sports; it's the nature of kids. We learn by falling and we survive by rising. It is a coach's worst nightmare to deal with an injured athlete. It's terrifying and it's traumatic and we hate seeing someone that we care for so much, be in pain.

I walked into competition and I thought I was on top of the world. We were the largest program there. For once, we were the big name. The team to beat.

When we let our pride take over, it's only a matter of time before we are reminded that pride comes before the fall. It is better to live humble than loud.

The week before our big National team travel trip out of town, at this little competition where we were the big name team- disaster struck. I asked one of my high level athletes to fill in on a lower level team for another girl who was running late.

It was a simple skill, a fill in request- nothing out of the ordinary. Yet, it became a day that will forever haunt me and never be remembered as ordinary at all.

A freak accident, a horrible mistake. As I hovered over her, arm shattered on the floor, I would've done anything to take the pain away. To turn the clock back and to not be in such a rush.

I will forever remember leaning over her and trying to comfort her, soothe her. The worst part was, that her main focus- the thing she was most upset about, was the fact she wouldn't be able to go on our big travel trip the next weekend.

Talk about humbling.

I will forever remember my necklace dangling in between us as she laid on the ground and I tried to keep calm over her and tell her I was so sorry for asking for to fill in. I will forever remember time standing still as I looked up and saw the girl- the girl who was running late- walking down the stairs towards us. What a difference a few minutes could have made.

Talk about haunting.

We lose sight of the little things; we get so caught up in winning, or being the big name, or looking the part that we so easily forget what's most important. We rush through life thinking that everything has to happen right now, in this instant. We have to fix every situation and have immediate remedies in our back pockets.

There's more to life than winning. In youth sports it's really easy to believe that our livelihood is based off of winning.

But it's not.

It's not winning at all. It's the special time we have together with athletes that we coach to leave an impact. You can't build a foundation on pride and you can't get a moment back.

Pride pushes perspective out the window. It is our job as coaches to hold onto perspective and use it to turn darkness into light — and Shine.

SEASON THREE
APRIL 2010

"Someone is sitting in the shade *today because someone planted a tree a long time ago."*

-Warren Buffett

Five years from now, I hope you look back and you're proud.

Proud to be a part of something from the beginning. Something you created. Something you believed in.

Not everyone has believed. People have looked down on us.
People have laughed at us. People have mocked us. People have told us we weren't good enough.

But you have fought back.

You were the ones that still wore a Shine shirt, ignored the rude comments, and never gave up on the bigger vision.

Five years from now, all of the little tiny cheerleaders will be the older athletes that a new generation is looking up to. And no one is going to laugh at them.
In five years- they will be the ones leading. They will be the kids who you have paved the way for.

You have to look at the legacy you are building as a tree. The younger athletes at the bottom, the older athletes closer and closer to the ends of the branches and leaves.

There comes a time when leaves fall off.

You move on, you go off to college, you grow up. Seasons change and people grow, but legacies last.

Those same leaves go back into the ground to help build upon the roots that they started out as. The tree just keeps growing bigger. Wherever the path leads, the roots we put down will undoubtedly help shape the future of cheerleading. That's the dream, that's the vision.

The impact you have is unstoppable, and I thank you for seeing the bigger picture even when it wasn't easy.

You have had a lot of disappointments and I wish I could take them away. I wish that you got first place every time, you deserve a gold trophy. There is no other group of kids that have bigger hearts and bigger dreams.

You are the believers. You are the kids that never gave up. You endured every struggle and every hardship, so years from now the path would be easy for the cheerleaders of tomorrow.

When you take the floor today, make it count. Cherish the memory and savor the moment. When you look back and remember this competition, what is it that you want to remember?

Remember that today marks the end of one season and tomorrow marks the beginning of a bigger future.

Sometimes I look around and I honestly don't know how we got here.

But I think it has something to do with believing...

SEASON THREE
APRIL 2009

The road that we have walked on over the past 2 ½ years has not been a smooth one. Our first year- our largest team lost every single competition. Not just lost- but came in dead last. It wasn't until their final competition, their last competition of the entire year that they finally won. I will never forget that moment. Every heartbreak and every loss was made up for in that one moment. It would have never been as sweet if they had won before. But to make their first win on that huge stage was amazing, and it was worth every loss.

Sometimes when things go wrong, it's easier to just give up or blame it on the circumstances. But everything that happens to us is to set up something for later on and let things fall into place. Every loss, every hurt, every disappointment- is the underlying reason for a good moment, a change, a new beginning. Setbacks create comebacks.

Shine was never easy to start and it still isn't easy. When Shine first opened- we didn't even have a real gym. Looking back- I know the only reason it worked and the only reason people stayed was because they believed in what Shine could be. They believed in the vision, they believed that in the end the good would win.

Every problem we have had, we have overcome. I truly believe that God is a Shine fan and I truly believe that Shine is meant to be here. We have gone through too much to not be still standing. We have had too many good things happen to us.

This is OUR now.

It's easy to say "It's not fair" and it's easy to point the finger and give up.

But it's the fight deep down inside me and you that keeps us growing and going.

Out of dark moments, flowers bloom.

"Go ahead, let the world ridicule our dreams and say
we're crazy.
It's usually the crazy ones who are crazy enough to change
the world, and the rest are either dumbfounded that we
managed to do so,
or so terrified that we will find a way to make our dreams a
reality."

- Unknown

SEASON FOUR LETTERS

"Keep away from people who try to belittle your ambitions.
Small people always do that,
but the really great make you feel that you, too, can become great."

-Mark Twain

SEASON FOUR
JULY 27, 2010

Three years ago, I turned the key, opened the door, and took a step into the journey of a lifetime.
I walked into an empty, half painted warehouse and had no idea what I was getting myself into.

It wasn't easy. It's been the hardest thing in the entire world.
Nothing can prepare you for opening a business. Especially a cheer gym.
It would be nice if it had come with a manual on how to do it- but it definitely doesn't.
At first the tears came easily, there were lots of ups and down.
I wanted everything to be perfect and everyone to be happy- but sometimes it doesn't always happen that way.
And the funny thing is- I thought I would be the one teaching- but I was actually the one who got to learn.

I have experienced the greatest joys and moments of happiness-
Seeing a kid who never thought they could accomplish a skill finally get it...
Watching a team come in last place all year and then finally be a National Champion First place winner at the last competition of the year
Watching kids come together and do whatever it takes to make it work...

And I've experienced the greatest heartbreak and challenges-
Watching a kid you love hit the floor and not get up,
seeing the disappointment when a team doesn't do as well as they

thought,
seeing the frustration of giving it your all and your all not being
enough as their all.

People never understood us.
We didn't have a lot of talent in the beginning; we didn't even
have a gym. And people always wondered why kids stuck
around.

Winning came as a rarity and it's taken a lot of hard work to
stand where we are today.
People would ask the older girls- why do you cheer at Shine?
They're so new; they're not even good yet.
And the girls would just shrug their shoulders and keep on.

Shine Athletics cheerleaders aren't a part of Shine Athletics- they
ARE Shine Athletics.
We created it together. They saw the big picture. They saw the
dream.
The girls who were juniors and seniors when Shine started and
are now in college- they didn't do it to cheer- they did it so your
kids could.
They knew someone had to start it- someone had to fail every
time so eventually someone else could succeed.
They saw the end of the road- so they did as much as they could
to get Shine started.

And now- as we enter our 4th season- everything we worked for
is finally coming to life.

I'm coaching the most talented teams I've ever seen.

There's not one team I would change. This is going to be our
year of dreams coming true. We've paid our dues.

   Our coaching staff is unbelievably talented and it's actually fun
to go to the gym with people I enjoy being around.

We don't just work together. We are friends. It's a support group that's indescribable. Through the good and the bad.

We have experienced some of the funniest inside jokes and best times together.
We have had to make some of the hardest decisions together and experienced the lowest of lows together as well.
Thank you for literally picking me up off the ground on those hard days. I owe each one of you the world.

I've never wanted Shine to be like any other gym, steal any one's kids, or spread anything but a love for cheerleading. We believe in trying to spread a love and acceptance for cheerleading and teaching kids to believe in themselves. At the end of the day- the most important things are not trophies, banners, or money. The most important thing in the entire world is relationships- it's about being there for people when they need you! It's hard to ask people for help. But at the end of the day- you have to surround yourself with things and people you would do anything for.

I was a 21 year old little girl with a big dream and I'll never forget the hurtful things that were done and said to try to stop me.
Most of it, surprisingly, came from adults.
It didn't make the process any easier, but it sure made us a lot stronger. I truly hope that no one ever does to your daughter what you did to me. I pray for y'all.

But more importantly than those who tried to bring me down, I will always remember the people who stood up for me and my idea.
The people who signed their kids up, passed out the flyers, and helped spread the word.
Those that painted the gym and moved in equipment in the dark, because we had no A/C or power.

The friends that wiped the tears away when things didn't go as planned and the people who pushed me to keep going.

The people that picked me up off the ground and said you will not quit. You will not give in. You will not give up and then forced me to keep going.

The kids that came back season after season, still hungry and ready to chase the dream.

Thank you.

It was never about cheerleading. It was about dreaming and being a dreamer.

Deep down inside of all of us are really big dreams.
Some too big to even say out loud. But that's what Shine represents- a really big dream; a really big possibility.
And at the end of the day- life is about the possibilities, not the guarantees. Because if we can do it- if Shine can make it- then maybe just maybe, dreams really do come true and maybe fairytales do come with a happy ending.

I used to look at every season as- are we going to make it?
But this season is different. We're on a different journey now.

So here's to the beginning of Season Four.
Here's to the past three years full of the good and bad.
Here's to the dreamers and the believers.
Here's to those that hurt us and made us stronger.
Here's to giving it all we've got.
And here's to every little girl with a really big dream.

Our belief will always be stronger than your doubt.

SEASON FOUR
DECEMBER 2010
EVENT PROGRAM BOOK

2nd Annual Full Circle Showcase

Wow!

Where to begin. First and foremost, THANK YOU for being here. This is truly a community event and I am so appreciative to be a part of a community as great as this one. Regardless of what color uniform we wear– we can come together for a great cause.

It's easy to hear the name Shine Athletics and think cheerleading. But to me, when I hear the name Shine Athletics– it's not about cheerleading at all. It's about dreaming and believing. Deep down inside all of us are really big dreams. Some too big to even say out loud. But that's exactly what Shine represents- a really big dream. A really big possibility.

And at the end of the day- life is about the possibilities, not the guarantees.

So take a second today- put aside the music, the uniforms, the clapping, and cheering– and take a look around. Fifteen different cheerleading teams in the same gym, for one reason. Bleachers packed with a community of support. The future is bright and the kids in this gym today are going to make the world a better place.

Today represents hopes and dreams. Today represents that the impossible, really is possible.

Today is our day to show you that dreams really do come true and fairy tales still come with a happy ending.

SEASON FOUR
JANUARY 2011

"You are allowed to fail without becoming a failure.
You're allowed to make mistakes without becoming one.
Hope can always be found again."

- Unknown

Everyone fails and everyone makes mistakes, yet we fear mistakes and most of us live in a constant state of a fear of failure.

Trying something new and taking a risk- even when it doesn't work out- isn't a failure. It's a learning experience and there's no better teacher than experience.

You might not always win, but you can never lose if you keep trying.

I think the only true mistakes we can make, are those actions we make without having good intentions.

They say karma always wins- and I am a firm believer that it does.
Sometimes it takes months, sometimes even years- but when you do things with good intentions, the good always comes back to you exponentially.

Don't ever be afraid to try something new and don't ever be afraid to take a leap of faith, it could lead you to the greatest things you've never imagined.

SEASON FOUR
FEBRUARY 2011

Throughout the history of Shine, there have been people who didn't get it.

They didn't believe in it and see the big picture and the possibility of what could be.

A lot of times, in life- when something happens to us- it's really hard to see the big picture. We get caught up in a moment, in a class at school, in a friendship, or in a relationship... and when something goes wrong or when someone disappoints us- we immediately act out. We make an angry comment or do something to try to get even or get the last word in.

But sometimes it's better to let fate fight our battles.

When Shine first opened and girls wore Shine shirts to school, they got made fun of.

Now, we have kids who don't even cheer at Shine, come in and buy shirts to wear.

The first season of Shine I had a team that lost every single competition.

They won their very last competition of the year.

I had a guy who absolutely HATED shine and did everything he could to try to take it down.

He now coaches at Shine every day, and would do anything to build Shine up.

The point is this:

There are things in your life that aren't going to work out. People are going to hurt you, make you mad, and disappoint you. Situations aren't always going to work out as you plan. You might find out that Mr. Perfect can't live up to his name. Maybe you won't get into your first choice college, or you'll lose a friend, or a job and you won't understand it. You'll struggle to understand it because- that's how you thought it was supposed to be.

I have had people leave the program and say hurtful things.
People have questioned if Shine would ever make it. If Shine would ever be successful. If Shine would ever win.

We will. We are. We did.

And we will continue to make it because we will never be those people. We will never be the doubters. We will never be the negative.
We will never teach our children to hate. We will teach our children to believe.

Remember, one loss doesn't end your story and one win can't complete it.
So tonight, let's continue to fight the good fight.

Fight the doubters and show the world what believing has always been about.

Our belief will always be stronger than their doubt.

SEASON FOUR
MARCH 2011

No coach in the world can guarantee a win.

Wait, what? Isn't that a Coach's job?

No. It's not a coach's job to guarantee a win. It's a coach's job to set a team up for a win through proper training, preparation, and making sure they're in a division and level that they are capable of competing at.

There comes a point in a season where there's nothing left to do as a Coach. Your athletes are trained, conditioned, ready, and disciplined. You have a great team but it is only when that team decides to be great that they truly can succeed.

It's kind of like when a Momma bird let's her baby birds take their first flight on their own. She can't do it for them. She's prepared them and nurtured them and given them the tools they need to succeed- but it's up to them to believe in themselves, use their wings, and really soar.

If you never push yourself, you miss the chance to see what you're really capable of. Everything you need is already inside of you. It's not about anyone else or any other team. It's not even about being the biggest or the best team, it's about being a team full of individuals who push themselves enough to create a greater team together.

A very wise person once told me that success comes from the heart, and it's more than true. When a team comes together and performs with giving it everything they can- not only can you see it; everyone can see it. Tomorrow, not only do I want to see it, but I want everyone that's there watching to see it too.

It's got to come from each one of you and each one of you has to give your 100 percent.

You got your wish to go to this competition and compete- now just believe in yourself and make your dream come true.

If everyone fights just a little bit harder, that adds up to exactly what you need to make it.

I believe in you all and I know you have what it takes.

Just remember- dream and believe, wishes come true.

SEASON FOUR
APRIL 2011

"For everything you have missed- you have gained something else"
-Unknown

Most of you know the story behind Shine. I coached for a recreational cheer program, and then decided to open a gym. Most of you have heard the story a million times. We started in a park. A middle school, a library. We had no air- no lights for weeks. We practiced in the heat, it was awful. Finally we got a gym. We grew. 4 teams. Boom. 5 teams. Boom. 6 teams to 7 and now here we are... not even 4 years later and we have 8 teams.

It's a story of perseverance and determination and never giving up. It's about believing. It's a Cinderella story. It truly is. And I hope when you look back at Shine that it is one of the main things you take away from it... Never, ever give up.

But most of you don't know the whole story. Actually, only two or three of you know it. So it is that time that I tell it. It's very dear to my heart and that is why I rarely share it. Here you go.

So many times, we miss out. We get hurt. We lose. And so many times we wonder why. Why us? Why did it have to have happen to me? We don't see it. We don't understand it.

10 years ago, I started coaching cheerleading as a volunteer for one reason. To get my scholarship to college. It was the only way I could go. I had to do it. And after three years of volunteer coaching, I was done- I accomplished my goals, coached a great group of kids, and headed off to college. I had big plans to go

and to never look back. It was a fresh start.

I wanted to make a difference- do something big with my life. And I looked at all these other people who I considered successful- they made it look so easy. I had my plan and I knew what I was going to do.

But sometimes, life has a different plan for you.

I got asked to coach a rec team again in college and I declined. I decided that I was ready to move forward and I just didn't have the time to be living out at college and commuting back to help coach. I told the Head coach I'd be happy to help out once in a while, but I just couldn't commit to being there full time. Three days before the first day of practice for the team I was asked to coach, my Mom had a major heart attack. She had to have open heart surgery and the recovery she was facing in front of her was really long.

When you get that call or walk into that hospital room, the pain is unbearable. You're not supposed to see the person that has always taken care of you as the person who now needs to be taken care of. Moms are supposed to be unstoppable and unbreakable; it's your Mom. It was my Mom. How could this happen to her? I was so angry. Out of all the people in the whole world- why MY Mom. She's so great, healthy and in shape- how could she have a heart attack? And why? She's such a great person... this shouldn't have happened to her.

I took care of her night and day for the next two to three weeks before she could even get back to walking normally and being able to do normal things like opening the refrigerator. I moved home. Cheerleading, life, college... nothing else really mattered at that point. It wasn't what I wanted to do- it was what I had to do.

About two weeks into my Mom's recovery, she asked me about cheer. She asked me if was going to be coaching again. I told her no and it was too late, the season had started. I had school starting back up and just didn't want to get involved coaching when the season had already started. However, my mom told me to go. It was only for two hours and she insisted that I needed to get out of the house. So I went. I didn't really want to, just because I was worried about leaving my mom at home- and I felt like I didn't even have the drive to coach anymore. So much had happened, the team had already started practicing and I didn't even know these kids.

When I walked into their practice, their second week as a team, I just watched them. I didn't know any of them- as I had missed the first week of practices but for some reason I felt drawn to helping them. The other coaches didn't seem very optimistic at their chances for a winning season and half the kids didn't even look like they knew what cheerleading was.

I wanted them to do good just because it seemed like no one thought they could. The day I met them I told them I would make them national champions. I told them that if they listened to me, I would take them to nationals and they would win. This team had never won anything before. Half of them were so scared of me I don't think they knew what to do with themselves; or maybe they just didn't even know what winning nationals meant.

With a large challenge ahead of me, I began my fifth year coaching cheerleading. I would take care of my mom during the days, do school online and then coach at night. I hated seeing my mom sick (doesn't everyone hate seeing their parents sick?) and cheerleading was an escape for me. None of the girls knew what was going on, so when I went to practice I just gave it all I had and threw 100% into that team. That team went on to get second place at nationals. They didn't win nationals- but they believed they could and that's what got them there. Believe it or not- the year I thought that cheerleading was over with for good was the year I decided to start a gym.

I don't tell a lot of people this story because it's personal. It's close to me and that's one of the reasons why Shine is so special to me. See people think I decided to open Shine… truth is, I didn't. The universe did it for me- I didn't have a choice. This was my fate- the struggle forced me to open my eyes and see what I needed to do. If something really bad didn't force me to come back here- I would have never had all of this. And it was a long process in the making. It took years for it to all play out- but it played out exactly as it was supposed to. That's why no one could stop it from happening.

You can't stop something that is meant to be and that is why even as young as I was when Shine opened- I knew I had to do it. That is why *believe* is so strongly used with Shine and why I always look for silly signs. I know, that deep deep down in my heart- this did not happen by accident. You are not reading this letter to forget it and you are not reading this letter just because you are a random cheerleader on a random all-star team. You were meant to be here, on this team- in this moment. Right here, right now. Years from now- you will look back and understand this moment and why you were a part of Shine. Maybe it's a friendship or a connection made, maybe it will be a lesson learned or a success that you celebrated.

Every time you think that a choice you make is causing you to lose something or miss out, you've got to hold on strong to the faith that you will gain something in its place… sometimes it just takes time to see it. For every disappointment or failure, the time will come for you to feel joy and happiness again, or a bigger success in return.

The things that you are struggling with now are things that will work out. I promise you, it really does get better. Sometimes it takes a weekend or a week, sometimes it's a month or a year. But the reasoning does come- you will look back one day and understand why the things in your life happen to you the way that they do.

Whether we realize it or not, the things that have happened to us in the past, happen to us to guide us along the right path to where we are supposed to be in our future. Every struggle and every discouragement- although we may not understand it- is how that season is supposed to play out at that time. You must believe that. And you must believe that no matter how bad it gets- you have to keep going.

If my mom had never had a heart attack, if I never had to move home and take care of her, if I had never had to endure that hurt and struggle, then I never would have had the best thing that ever happened to me.

"When darkness comes and fear fills your heart, know, there is a way.

When all your dreams come crashing down, know, there is a way. When friends cannot be found and there is no one to comfort you, know, there is a way.

When you are ready to lay down and quit, know, there is a way.

To know is to find the way. Knowing cannot be found out there.
Knowing is found in the silence of surrender within.

The way is within."

- John McIntosh and Reverend Polito

SEASON FIVE LETTERS

*"I'll never regret the things I've done.
I've got too much left to say and too much to
become."*

-Alex Gaskarth

SEASON FIVE
JULY 27, 2011

Life is funny.

I guess you could say that oftentimes, the universe has a sense of humor.

It gives us what we want, but sometimes in the ways we never see coming.

July 27, 2007 was the most exciting day of my life. I officially, with a permit, was able to walk into our gym. FINALLY making the reality happen.

But look at that same date only a couple years earlier.

July 27, 2005. The scariest day of my life. I walked into the hospital and they told me my Mom wasn't going to make it.

That was the day the universe conspired to show me that it had a much greater plan in mind for me.

It was a day that I thought would forever be engraved in my brain as the worst day of my life. I date I would dread. A day I would fear as the calendar rolled toward it every year.

But it's not. I love July 27th.

A date that I thought I would resent every year has become a day that fills me with gratitude every year.

I am so grateful to still have my Mom.

I am so grateful to be a part of something as wonderful as Shine.

It often takes many years and a good deal of hindsight to realize that bad dates don't have to always mean bad days forever.

Disappointments will always happen, even to good people. But every day we have the power to continue to believe in something greater, a plan, and a purpose. We have the choice every day to create positive in our lives and to keep moving forward.

Bad things aren't breaking points that hinder you from reaching your dreams, they are redirections towards something greater.

When one dream doesn't come true, trust that the universe is lining up something better for you that you never saw coming. It'll still sting, it'll still break your heart, and it'll still hurt- but you have to hold on to the belief that you'll never miss out on what's truly meant for you and the holes in your heart will one day be filled.

SEASON FIVE
OCTOBER 2011

During the first season of Shine, I searched for a photographer to come to the gym to take gym pictures of all of the teams. I did some homework online and found a photographer from South Florida who worked with a ton of gyms and from what I could see, took great team pictures.

He also did live photos at almost all of the Florida competitions. I reached out and luckily was able to schedule a time for him to come in and do all of our photos right after our brand new uniforms were scheduled to arrive.

It felt like everything was coming perfectly together.

The photographer came in November and promised everyone the pictures would arrive before Christmas. He was great! I remember everyone being so excited, including myself; the uniforms and the pictures made it real.

Fast forward to the week leading up to Christmas and no pictures had arrived. According to the photographer, the first shipment had been delayed and the second shipment burned down in a shipping truck fire. Seriously, this is what I was told. The pictures exploded on the back of a truck.

Not only did I have disappointed and angry customers who had trusted me to provide a trustworthy photographer but I was extremely disappointed as well. And to be honest, I didn't really know what to do. It was the first big issue I had working with another business vendor and I just didn't know how to even handle the situation or this man who was well established as a photographer in the cheer industry.

After weeks of being ignored and well after the Holidays had gone by, I was told by the photographer that I needed to realize my gym didn't matter to him. I was a small gym that barely made him any money and it would cost him more to reprint my pictures than he actually made off of them in the first place. He assured me though that the pictures would arrive (eventually) and that he hoped one day he would be the photographer capturing the moment of my gym winning at a competition. (Ouch.)

He made me feel so small. He made me feel like I would never be a relevant customer to him or a big enough gym to actually matter. He told me that gyms like mine come and go all the time.

Towards the end of February, the photos finally arrived and at our last event of the season, he was working the competition and taking the pictures there all day. He came up to me at one point, shoved a CD in my hand and told me it contained the remaining pictures he owed me. Maybe that was his way of trying to make things right.

Over the past five years, I have seen this man time and time again at multiple different competitions. Every time I see him, I remember the way he made me feel. We make eye contact and I know he remembers too.

There was never an apology or even a justification for all of his excuses. Intentions do matter and words can't be taken back after they are said or sent in writing.

Last season, when I tried to start a dance program at Shine it failed miserably. And it wasn't for a lack of talent.

I had the most talented group of dancers that I had ever seen, these kids were so hard working and they all loved to dance. The problem was, I didn't take the time to build a foundation. I didn't have the right people in the right places to grow a love of dance into a long lasting dance program.

I tried to produce quick and immediate results to compete with another dance program when I should have been focused on creating a solid foundation for something to grow.

I went into it focused on competition. I started a dance program just to compete, not because my heart was in it.

When you focus on what everyone else is doing and you try to keep up with them, all you end up doing is chasing. You lose sight of what you really wanted in the first place. You lose sight of YOUR passion and your goals because you're constantly comparing what you have to everyone else.

What works for you and what feels like to success to you is not going to look or feel like success to everyone else. And it's very rare that short term work will yield long term results.

Overnight success is imaginary. Success is created behind the scenes. Success is the years of work that go into something that no one knows about. I knew that, because that's how Shine started.

But I guess I needed a reminder and to learn that lesson the hard way.

When you try to take a short cut to success, you miss out on the joy in creating something of your own. Is something really worth having if you have it for the wrong reasons?

Over the course of six months or so, I watched the dance program that I had so desperately tried to throw together (just to one up someone else) crumble into the ground.

The situation with the dance program reminded me a lot of the photographer. At first, I was really scared to take accountability and admit that I made a mistake. But I never wanted to be like that photographer. Excuse after excuse after excuse.

I had to take accountability for my mistakes and own up to it.

I refunded a lot of money and gave a lot of apologies to those that were a part of the dance program. It didn't work out, and although it may have been easier to point the finger and say it was because the dance coach quit, or we had to get a new coach, or practices changed days- the truth is it didn't work out because I didn't invest the right amount of time into making it a sustainable and solid program in the first place.

Sometimes, as much as we don't want to, we fail. We let people down. We make promises we can't keep. But we always have the decision to own up to our actions. To try to make it better. To try to restore our word.

I've said things and done things that I wish I hadn't. But my memories of this photographer will always remind me that the way we treat people is the way we are remembered. Roadblocks, mistakes, and failures are a part of life. They shape us, and if we let them- they shape us into better people.

We don't always make the right decisions. But we can always try to make our decisions right.

SEASON FIVE
NOVEMBER 2011

"What is normal for a spider is chaos for the fly."

- Charles Addams

We used to have a white leather couch in Shine. I don't really remember how it got there, but it did a great job of creating a small, yet effective, athlete break area. Yes, that's all we really had room for- just a couch- to serve as a break area. It got shuffled around a few different times and over time, it seemed to get closer and closer to the door- and closer and closer to being out the door and into the garbage.

Towards the end of the life of the white couch, when it had been pushed into the furthest side corner of the gym, it was still being used by the older athletes. They would come to the gym straight from high school and use it to complete their homework, or talk, or hangout before practice.

Everyone else in the gym thought it was a waste of space, a now faded white leather, cracked couch. However, the day before the couch was scheduled to be sent to the trash it fulfilled its purpose.

I noticed one of the girls walk into the gym, no eye contact, shoulders slumped over, and looking extremely upset. I watched for a few moments as she walked directly to the couch, slammed her backpack down, and wiped her tears.

I waited a minute or two and then walked over. I sat down next to her and asked what was going on.

"My Mom," she said tearfully, without eye contact. "My Mom just hates me," she choked out.

I gasped a little, as I knew for sure this was the furthest thing from true, but was still shocked to hear she felt this way.

"No, of course she doesn't" I told her and asked her to explain to me what happened.

As the conversation progressed, she told me how she believes her Mom blames her for her Dad leaving and the reason her Mom and Dad are no longer together is because of her.

Family issues are hard. Hard to understand and even harder to accept. My Dad left when I was little and I haven't heard from him since. Although I don't know what it's like to watch your parents go through a divorce, I know what it's like to wonder what happened; especially when it comes to a situation where someone abandons their responsibilities as a parent.

I told her, repeatedly, that adult relationships are something that kids should never try to understand. It's never a child's fault when a divorce happens. It's never a child's job to try to put pieces back together and solve a problem that they had no part in creating.

After consoling her and explaining to her that adult problems cannot be saved or caused by a child- she said one last thing to me that really struck home.

"I just want to have a normal family. All of my friends have normal families and I'm the only one who doesn't."

Another statement that felt so true to my heart, in that moment, my heart hurt with hers.

I used to be so embarrassed that I only had a Mom. It always seemed like there were Dad events I was missing out on. A Father Daughter dance, a Dad walking his daughter down the homecoming court aisle, a Dad who would at least even send a birthday card.

I was embarrassed that I didn't have the normal.

I always thought my family life wasn't good enough because it didn't look like anyone else's. I just wanted the normal picture of family that I had painted in my head.

Looking back, I wish someone would have told me that normal doesn't last. Normal doesn't really even exist. Everyone's family is different- and that's okay.

I now look back and feel blessed to have been raised differently, blessed to have had an example of a single, working Mother. It is because of those differences, that I am who I am today. I don't think my story would be the same and I don't think I would be where I am now if I had been raised any differently.

Don't be afraid to embrace your differences from everyone else- it is your story and your story alone that can help show others the light at the end of the tunnel.

It doesn't matter where you come from, you can grow up to create the world you want and the dreams that you believe in. Who you are today does not dictate where you can go tomorrow. You have the power to overcome any set of circumstances that become a road block in your path.

You are not alone and if you're reading this, I guarantee that someone out there wishes they had a life like yours. Appreciate what you have and remember that what you see as normal, someone else sees as different.

**SEASON FIVE
DECEMBER 2011
EVENT PROGRAM BOOK**

3rd Annual Full Circle Showcase

Wow!

THANK YOU for being here. This is truly a community event and I am so appreciative to be a part of a community as great as this one. Regardless of what color uniform we wear– we can come together for a great cause.

Showcase is my absolute favorite event of the entire year because it's the one time we get to see our kids fully enjoy their performances without the pressure and stress of competition or a trophy. It's about making a memory and leaving an impact on what we have accomplished together in the community. Showcase means everything to us at Shine- and I hope when you walk into Showcase today you see the magic behind it and take pride that you have had a hand in creating something that means so much to so many people. I know it's easy to get caught up the hair/ makeup/ will the stunt hit/ does the uniform fit/ etc., but that's not what today is about. Today is truly just about enjoying the accomplishments and hard work of the past six months.

Our kids have been working so hard to put these routines together and I hope you use today to look at the growth, the development, the accomplishments, and the journey that has led us up to this event. It's not about perfection. It's not about being THE best... it's not a competition. It's about the athletes being THEIR best.

So take a second today- put aside the music, the uniforms, the clapping, and cheering– and take a look around. Twenty three different cheerleading teams in the same gym, for one reason. Bleachers packed with a community of support.

The future is bright and the kids in this gym today are going to make the world a better place.

Today represents hopes and dreams. Today represents that the impossible, really is possible. Today is our day to show you that dreams really do come true and fairy tales still come with a happy ending.

At the end of the day, the most important things in life are not bought, they are built. And Showcase is something we have built together.

Together we believe; together we can make a difference.

SEASON FIVE
JANUARY 2012
E-MAIL TO: ALL

First of all, CONGRATULATIONS to everyone at Shine Athletics! Today was truly a historic day!

Today we took 5 out of our 9 teams to competition in Lakeland and every single Shine team won first place.

For the first time ever, we *swept* the competition. Five first places, what a HUGE accomplishment.

Our teams look better than ever. They are clean, they are sharp, and they are hard to beat! From a coaching perspective, you can't ask for much more.

We challenge each child to give their team their personal best, and today was exactly that!

However, looking back at today, today wasn't just about winning. It was about being a part of something that you've built; something you can call your own.

A few times throughout the day, I saw a butterfly flying in the building around the competition.

After the awards ceremonies, they ushered everyone off the stage super quick. We barely had time to take pictures.
And as we were walking away- for a moment, the entire stage was clear.

It was one of those moments where everything stops for a split second so you can make it a memory- and in that split second, I swear I saw the butterfly fly right across the backdrop one last time.

And I know it was a butterfly.

I heard other people laugh and say it was a moth or a bird or a bug.
But I know it was a butterfly. And really, regardless of what it was, the important thing is what we believed it was.

Many times, things have to be believed before they can be seen. Which is a very true statement when it comes to Shine and our past cheer seasons. We have always had kids and parents who believed that today would happen. Our kids today are sitting in the shade, from the trees that the kids and parents of our past planted for us many years ago. The past four years can be looked at as the caterpillar. And a caterpillar doesn't become anything more than what it started out as without a struggle. We have had many mistakes, lessons to learn, and we've lost many times. But today, Shine got to become the butterfly. As a whole, our entire program has grown and blossomed into something really great, just like a butterfly. Shine has truly been built by every single person who has walked in and out of its doors.

Today doesn't mean we will win every competition in the future. It doesn't mean we're the best in the whole world, untouchable or unbeatable.

Today represents a vision and a belief of what is possible. Today is a stepping stone to many greater things lying ahead for all of us at Shine.

Whether you have been at Shine for the past four seasons or the past three weeks, I hope the message is clear:

When you come to Shine, it doesn't matter what you once were. It matters what you believe you can be.

At the end of the day, I couldn't be happier with our wins today.

I'm still smiling. And even though Shine Athletics is a competitive cheerleading gym, it's really not just about win or lose. It's not really even about cheerleading, because at the end of the day- cheerleading will always just be cheerleading. Anyone can call themselves a cheerleader, but only the lucky ones get to call themselves believers. Shine will always be something that you got to build and be a part of. Years from now, when all our current cheerleaders are done cheering, and grown up and doing great things-- they aren't going to remember winning today. But they will remember being a part of something that made them believe that anything is possible. And one day- years from now, when someone else sees a bird or bug or moth, our girls will see a butterfly.

Success isn't winning; success is the fact that one symbol, one word, one belief, and one cheer can mean SO much, to so many.

SEASON FIVE
FEBRUARY 12, 2012

Three years ago, at this very competition I will never remember being more excited. I had briefly lost my mind and decided to bring our half season team to State Fair. Yes, the half season team that started in January, I had scheduled to compete a month later- in February. It was a huge group of girls. We had 32 girls I'm pretty sure- and they were all young. It was our first half year youth team and we had so much talent on the team, we went Large Youth 2.

I worked for hours, HOURS- making charts and planning out exactly how to run their practices in order for them to have a full choreographed routine by State Fair. Eight full practices and maybe one extra Saturday…. Was it possible? To really take a half year team and put them on the floor in a month?

Well, call me crazy, but we did it. State fair competition came around and I was so excited to show off our large half season team. I was so proud to be the only gym around that had so many kids come for half year and that we were able to put a routine together that quickly.

Three teams in the division. We came in third place, last place, to two other great teams.

To me, all I could see was the good. I didn't really care that we had just "lost" because I was so proud of how hard the kids had worked. I didn't really care that the other two teams beat us as year round teams, since we had only practiced for a month. And we didn't even lose bad- we were half a point away from second place! Half a point! I thought this was an accomplishment. I thought this was such good progress for a young group of new cheerleaders.

I knew a few of the parents weren't happy that they had lost, but I tried to explain that it was half year and it was only their first competition. At the next competition, the team got 2nd out of 3 teams and had an even better performance. The kids were learning new skills and the routine looked better and cleaner.

After the second competition, I started hearing talk of a group of kids and their parents leaving to go to another gym. These types of rumors happen often and I wasn't really worried about it, because their kids seemed to absolutely love cheerleading- and to absolutely love Shine.

Well the week before the season was ending, four of the girls and their parents went to another gym's practices. They started telling everyone that they were leaving to go to this other gym- AND they were trying to get other people to leave with them!

Finally I had to say something. I asked one of the mothers of the cheerleaders what was going on, I asked her if it was true. This woman looked me square in the eye and told me this:

"We want to win. Shine is never going to win. We're not really even sure if you're going to make it and last. And if we're going to invest in our child's cheerleading future, we want to cheer at a gym that wins."

That was three years ago, however when someone says something like that to you- it sticks. It's not something that you forget and it's not something that I haven't worried about. I cried for a week straight wondering if this woman was right. What if we never won? What if Shine never won? What if we didn't ever make it?

For a week straight I just felt like a failure and I wanted to stop coaching. I was so upset over what this woman said to me about Shine. I wanted to write her a mean email or prank call her house or really just do anything to make her feel some sort of pain that I was feeling. I wanted so badly to prove her wrong.

Now, truth be told- after that- we didn't start winning all the time. We didn't have a miracle shine down on us from the heavens and we didn't win every competition the next season or even the next after that. Life went on as usual, new kids came to Shine, that family went to the rival gym (with a few others), and we continued to grow and get better.

A few months after she left the program, I had pulled into a local grocery store and I recognized this woman's white SUV parked in the parking lot. As I walked through the parking lot, I froze behind her vehicle. On her back window, where there had previously been a megaphone with the word Shine underneath of it pressed into the glass, there was now the name of the new gym she had joined- placed over the scratched out letters of the Shine sticker that was once there and that had left a lasting impression on the glass.

Part of me wanted to chase her down in that store and give her a piece of my mind. Instead, I turned around and walked back to my car as the lump in my throat began to grow. It was one of those images that stuck in my brain and bothered me for the rest of the night. It was almost like the universe was reminding me of this woman's cruelty and harshness. *You'll never make it* are difficult words to be told. Part of me wanted so badly to tell her the gym was doing well, I wanted the last word. However, I didn't get it. I never chased her down. I never ran after her. I cried in my car in the parking lot of a grocery store and after that, I never spoke to her other than a simple hello in passing as the years went by.

Three years after she left, three years later, a Shine team beat the team that this woman's daughter was cheering on. Not only beat, but won first place.

We finally had a team in the same division and we finally won. It was huge, it was loud and it was out in the open so everybody could hear it and see it.

At the end of the day, as I walked to my car to go home, I saw the woman- the same woman who told me I would never win- walking with her daughter to go home, in the parking lot. I saw her. I replayed a flashback of her doubt, I remembered her words, and I remembered the way it made me feel. I was a few feet behind them so I had a full on view of the two of them climbing into that white SUV with the same scratched out Shine sticker still on the back of it that I stood behind in a grocery store parking lot three years ago. But this time, as I walked past the vehicle it was different. I smiled. I smiled because it was the moment of vindication and the moment of my fears and doubts about ever being able to "make it" and "win" finally being erased.

I truly believe that there is a plan for all of us and sometimes it's just really, really hard to see it. You just have to keep believing that there is a master plan on your side. You might not get the payoff today or tomorrow- but the things that are meant for you and your life WILL happen. Good things will HAPPEN TO YOU. Because when you live with passion and follow your heart and do what is right, good things do come back to you. When you give the world the best you have, the best does come back to you.

The next time someone says something mean or hurts you- don't serve your own dish of revenge. Let the Universe do it. Because the Universe can serve it so much better and bigger than you ever imagined. Spend your time on making yourself better, not on being bitter.

In the end, fate always wins. No matter how great something is or how bad something gets- if it's meant to be, then fate will make it be.

You can't stop something that is truly meant to be.

Instead of spending your time trying to get the last word- speak a little kinder, be a bit nicer, and stay silent instead of saying a rude comment back to someone.

Why would you want to get the last word, when you can get the last laugh?

"Change is the essence of life.
Be willing to surrender what you are for what you could
become."

-Reinhold Niebuhr

SEASON FIVE
APRIL 11, 2012
E-MAIL TO: ALL

Dear Shine Families,

A big thank you to everyone who came to the parent meeting tonight- This email is going to relay the information from tonight's parent meeting.

First and foremost, I want each one of you to know that writing this email is extremely bittersweet. Shine has been my entire life and my entire world for the past 5 years of my life. In everything I have done at Shine, I have truly tried to do things the "right" way- I committed do right by the people who have been loyal and committed to Shine- and I wanted every choice to be one that people would understand, accept, and respect. It has been the greatest five years of my life and I wouldn't change a thing about it.

As many of you know, we have been working very hard to plan for the future of Shine. As part of that plan, we put much thought into relocating to a new building. We were very excited about the possibility of moving into the front building in our current plaza, but unfortunately after looking at the rent pricing with taxes and overhead- it's not something we would be able to do financially. After evaluation the numbers and careful consideration, we realize it was simply not possible for our business and that it wouldn't be in the best interest of our members.

We searched extensively for a new location/building that would provide us with what we felt was necessary for Shine to continue progressing. Unfortunately, we could not find a facility that provided both the space and the affordability that we require. We realized that this was not the right time for us to move into a new building and we were prepared to spend the next year in our current location. I say all of this to assure you that the talk of a new gym and the hype surrounding the move was 100% genuine and our excitement was authentic.

Over the past few years, there have been conversations between myself and our soon to be partners. Those conversations have been very open to the possibility of a potential merger of the two gyms. This is something that both parties have been open to; however, over the past couple years we have not been able to find a middle ground in order to both do what we felt was best for our people.

Recently, both parties have decided to reopen discussions and work together to create something that would truly be great for you and your child.

Please understand that this is not a decision that we have come to lightly. It is not without much thought and prayer and careful consideration that we have arrived at this place. I would not be okay with this if I did not have each of you and your best intentions in mind. I would not be satisfied with the decision we have made if I had any doubt that you would not ultimately benefit from the result.

The Daytona Beach competition on April 21st will be the last competition for both programs under their current names. Effective in May, with the start of team placements- we will relocate and start the new inaugural season with our unified new name and brand.

Speaking to the logistics of the merger, I want it to be clear that this combination considers the members of both programs as absolute equals in this arrangement. I want everyone to know that this combination would not be happening if it was not on equal terms. Every Shine staff member and coach is on board and a part of this merger. Our biggest goal is to make this transition as easy as possible for YOU and your child. This is going to be a positive environment and everyone is going to feel welcome.

This program is the beginning to an extremely great future for cheerleading in our area. We have done everything possible to ensure that this new gym will truly honor and respect both cheerleading gyms and be able to offer the absolute best cheerleading possible.

There is so much to gain from this combination. We are all truly excited for a new season, new teams, and to have so much talent under one roof. I am so excited to finally squash this rivalry between our two programs as well. Both gyms have created their own legend and left a legacy that will long be remembered- instead of spreading animosity to our children, it's time we come together to appreciate what both gyms and staffs have to offer. I want our coaches and staff members to be remembered as leaders- and this is what leaders do: They work together and come together and do what is best for a group of people as a whole. Leaders are able to look at the big picture and set realistic long term goals- and for you and for our community as a whole, this is what is best.

Although after Daytona, we may not see the name "Shine" across a uniform top anymore- this is not the end of a beautiful legacy. Shine is a sparkling memory that only the lucky ones have to say they got to be a part of. Shine will live on in the absolute best way possible- as a success, as a dream and most importantly proof that a little girl with a really big dream can make a difference. I was 21 years old when I opened Shine and when I have the time to write it all down, it's going to be an amazing story. We've had an amazing run and an amazing five years. I'm very proud to say that we are going out on top. Shine was exactly what a dream should be. We did it the right way and Shine's journey has truly been fulfilled. We made it.

For every butterfly you see, I hope you remember what it's like to grow up with the real life magic that Shine truly was and will forever be.

For every little girl with a really big dream, I hope you smile and tell her she really can do it.
And if you've never believed before- I hope you do now.

Our new gym is going to be incredible. It is going to be an amazing cheerleading gym. We are ready. We are prepared. With belief in our hearts- we are ready to be that MEGA cheer gym.

It is our central goal to make these next two weeks special for your child. I know you will have lots of questions and this email does not answer them all. All of the necessary information will soon be forthcoming; however, right now we need to focus on the kids. I need your help in making these next two weeks special for them. We want our last competition to be full of happy memories, celebrating the accomplishments our kids have had this season, and lots of pictures to look back on! After Daytona, we are going to have the absolute best end of season banquet EVER! I need your help and I need your support at this time to make this about our kids. We are shaped by the light that we let through us- and it is time to pass on what Shine has given to us, to other people. Some How It'll Never End.

Don't stop believing; because believing is only the beginning.

With all my love,
Sydney

SEASON FIVE
APRIL 21, 2012
Some How It'll Never End

What is Shine Athletics?

From the outside looking in- I don't think you can ever understand it. From the inside looking out- I don't think you could ever fully explain it.

Today may be the last cheerleading competition for Shine, but it is not the end of Shine. Therefore, anyone who feels that this is the end must have missed what Shine really was.

Shine is not a warehouse. Shine is not a uniform top. Shine was never just a cheerleading gym. It had to start that way to create a message and purpose of what it is truly supposed to be.

It's a dream, a passion, a fire lit deep down inside of you.
It's yours and it is you. It's in your hands to do something great with the Shine legacy now.

Towards the end of one of my favorite movies, a girl is crowned the Spring Queen of her school. She works really hard to win the crown and even sabotages others chances of winning. But, at the end, when she wins the crown she realizes it doesn't really matter in the grand scheme of things. A crown is a nice thing… but if you're not enough without a crown- you'll never be enough with one. And so she breaks the crown into pieces and she throws them into the crowd, because she wants everyone to have a piece and everyone to take something away from getting a part of the crown.

Well, that's how I see Shine today. I am giving a piece of it to each and every one of you. And the only people who can keep the dream alive and pass it on to others and pay it forward- is YOU. Shine is yours now. Shine is YOU.

Success is not a trophy. Or a crown. Or any material object. Like I said above, if you're not enough without it- you'll never be enough with it. And you are enough. You have more than enough deep down inside of you to do great things. Some of the amazing things that are planned for your life are things you have not even imagined yet. The future for you is going to be so great and you are going to do so many amazing things. My heart is happy and so full today because YOU got to live Shine to the fullest and YOU will be the reason that it continues to live on.

There's a story I love that basically explains the process of a caterpillar turning into a butterfly.

The story talks about a man who is watching a butterfly attempt to emerge from its cocoon. He's watching and nervous because there's a tiny little hole and it appears that the butterfly isn't going to make it out. So the man decides to help the butterfly and cut the cocoon open. The butterfly then emerges easily. But it has a swollen body and small, shriveled wings. The man continues to watch the butterfly because he expects it to just spread its wings and fly away.

But it never happens.

The butterfly ends up never looking like a real butterfly. It stays small and shriveled, and has to spend the rest of its life crawling around.

What the man didn't realize was that the struggle required for the butterfly to get out of the cocoon is the struggle that prepares the butterfly for what's next.

The struggle is what gives the butterfly strength.

The struggle is what prepares the butterfly for what lies ahead.

The point is: sometimes struggles are exactly what we need in our life. If we went through life without any obstacles, we wouldn't be living. Without a struggle once in a while we would never grow and become stronger.

And we could never fly...

When you look at Shine as a cocoon or a starting place, you have an advantage that no one else has. You know what it's like to struggle and to work hard for something. You know what it's like to overcome any obstacle. You know how to lose and you know how to win— and that is a lesson that many people miss out on. Today, you get to be the butterfly and emerge stronger and ready for anything and for your journey. Whatever that may be- it's yours to decide and yours to live out fully.

Remember, your journey won't look like everyone else's. And someone else's success is not your failure. We all have our own paths to walk and our own versions of success.

I talk a lot about fairy tale endings... but I have to say, this is not one.

This is now your story to tell. You can follow your dreams with Shine always on your side and always in your heart. You can let the dream live on and pass the dream on to others.

Shine is not ending today. It is actually truly just beginning.
You see, that's what Shine really stands for:
Some **H**ow **I**t'll **N**ever **E**nd.

It's time to show the world what believing is all about. It starts right here and it starts right now. One last performance and then it is in your hands what happens next.

I am always here for you and I will always believe in you.
Get ready to change the whole world for the better.
I'll be watching with pride.

"In the end, what matters is not so much what you bought, but what you built; not so much what you got, but what you shared; not so much your success but your significance; not so much your competence, but your character; not so much what you said, but what you did."

-Michael Josephson

THE LAST LETTER

"We lose ourselves in the things we love.
If we're lucky, we can find ourselves there too."
                                                    - Unknown

THE LAST LETTER
APRIL 25, 2012

This letter is a little different. This letter is to me, if I could write myself a letter when I was 18. But this letter is also to you, you just might not understand everything in it quite yet. This is the one letter I hope you keep- when you're going through a hard time or something you just don't understand and all you want to do is look in a crystal ball and find the answer and see that everything turns out okay- I hope you remember this letter. I hope this letter gives you peace and I hope it gives you hope. And most importantly I hope it reminds you of how much I love every single one of you.

Dear (18 year old) Sydney,

You're going to run away to college and want to never look back. You're going to dream about moving away and making a huge impact on people's lives. College is going to be great- it's really not as scary as it seems now. It's time that you leave the comfort zone of home and high school and move on to your next chapter and adventure. Everyone has to do it, enjoy it. Go out a little more, worry a little less, and don't neglect your friendships.

Your world is going to get shaken to the core. Something you never expected is going to happen. It's going to be extremely scary and life changing. But it's going to be the catalyst to the best thing that ever happened to you. It's going to bring you back home. Be a little nicer to your Mom, you'll look back and wish you had spent more time with her.

You're going to go back to something that you swore you wouldn't. Coaching cheer. You're going to hate going back to it at first, because you're going to feel like you're missing out on fun and parties and college. Fun and parties and college don't last- ten years from now it's not going to matter that you got in the club for free because you knew the door guy. Popularity fades, kindness does not.

A vision, a lightbulb, a dream is going to light up in your head. It's going to be the best thing that ever happens to you. It's going to be scary and hard and life changing- but it's going to be YOURS. Your dream- and no one can ever take that away from you.

You're going to plan it for a year or so, and try so hard to get it right. There are going to be times when it looks hopeless- but don't give up. There are going to be people who betray you, friends who make fun of you, grown adults who tell you that you can't do it—don't listen to them. Jealously is an ugly thing.

You're going to promise yourself that you are following this dream for the right reasons. It's not about fame, or money, or winning anything- it's something you're going to build for the people you love. And you're going to promise yourself that the day it changes and the day it becomes about status, money, or winning, you'll get out. Don't forget that promise.

People are going to crucify you for every mistake. You are going to threaten the livelihood of someone in the same business as you- and some of the things she is going to do to you are going to be very mean. You are going to worry she will destroy your chances at making it.

She won't.

There are going to be people who you think are on your side and they are going to turn on you and tell you awful things.

Someone that you trust is going to promise you business and help with your business, and instead she is going to take her kids and her friends to a rival business instead. A woman you trusted is going to tell you that you will never win a competition. Don't listen to her- because you will and one day you will even beat the very team that her child is on. Time is a funny thing- it won't happen overnight and you won't see the light at the end of the tunnel right away- but all of the people that hurt you, you will understand it one day.

Don't retaliate against the negative. The way people treat you is their karma. The way you react, is yours. Don't try to get the last word in- you will get the last laugh one day.

There is going to be a rival coach that gets under your skin to the point that you want to quit. He's going to make you feel like you don't want to do this anymore, and he's going to try really hard to make you break. But one day, he's going to need you. And when he does- believe him that he is being genuine and don't give him such a hard time. He's going to change your whole life and push you to be the absolute best you can be. He gets it.

Don't neglect the good people- because they will always outweigh the bad people. You mean a lot to people- be positive and be a leader. You have the world in your hands.

This dream isn't going to last forever but it's going to be exactly what you need it to be at this time period in your life. It's going to teach you responsibility, accountability, and teamwork. It's going to give you the best resume and business experience you could ever ask for. It's going to make you pray to God that you make it and it's going to humble you to your knees when you make mistakes. It's going to teach you how to grow up and most importantly it's going to teach you about love.

You are going to love this dream more than anything you have ever loved. And you're not going to realize that until it nears an end. You're going to struggle with relationships and you're going to constantly ask yourself why it's not working out with this guy or that guy. You're going to get your heart broken really bad. Really bad. And it's going to hurt so bad. All you're going to want is your fairytale ending... But the truth is- you love your dream so much, that you aren't really ready to love anything else the way you love your dream. You are living a fairytale. A dream that so many will never get to live. You're going to give your whole heart to a group of people who believe in what you believe in. And that's okay. Because love will find you and for right now, this is what you are meant to do and these people and this dream is the love that you need to give.

As you get older, you're going to start to get that itch again. The itch of a new possibility, a new beginning. That wonder of "what if"... and that's okay. The kids you built your dream for are going to grow up too. No one is going to hate you for wanting to start a new chapter and build a new dream. You built the walls and only you get the choice to bring them down.

When you decide what has to be done- it's going to take a big hit to your pride. You're going to have to give up what you know for the unknown. You are going to be terrified and devastated and sad and scared. It will be okay. A new door will open. The phone didn't ring the day you needed it to as a coincidence. God is going to give you an open door and an opportunity to discover yourself in a brand new way.

And you want to know, deep down, what your biggest fear is going to be? It's going to be hurting people that have supported you. You're going to be petrified that people are going to hate you. You're going to stay up sleepless nights to try to figure out how to tell people about your next step. And that proves that you lived your dream for the right reasons. And anyone who doesn't understand or gives you a hard time- one day they will understand.

It takes a lot of courage to release the familiar and seemingly secure, to embrace the new. But there is no real security in what is comfortable. There is more security in the adventurous and exciting, for in movement there is life, and in change there is power.

Don't be afraid to fail- because I promise you never, ever will.
Tell people how much they mean to you and don't be afraid to take a chance.

Let's face it- you don't have all the answers. But remember, neither does anyone else, and that in a way, is your advantage. You are on an equal playing field. Stop focusing on what you don't have, because you have all you need. You're going to pray for insight and for someone to show you a picture of your future- so you can have peace of mind that everything works out for you in the end.... But if you could have seen what the next 8 years were going to be- you wouldn't have believed how lucky you would be... how lucky you are.

As you close one door- just keep in mind that somehow, it'll never end.
"Some How It'll Never End"
Those 5 words are going to change your whole life.

And always, always remember-- Believing is only the beginning.

Love,
Sydney

"The dream was always running ahead of me.
To catch up, to live for a moment in unison with it,
that was the miracle."

- Anais Nin

AFTERWORD
JULY 27, 2012

Do you ever close your eyes and in an instant, slow blink of the eye, get taken back? It's like the entire world is still rushing, still spinning, still swirling all around you, but you're frozen in this perfect bubble of a memory, a daydream maybe, but it takes you right back to that moment of greatness?

That second of time where you can see the people around you and you can literally hear your own heart beat back in that moment while every other sound seems to be a blurred background noise.

With a single inhale you can once again smell the true magic that was lingering in the air and takes you back inside of that place you once were.

Sometimes it's a song, or lyric, or even a melody that can wrap you right back inside of that moment that is now a memory.

How can something that lasted for five years be seen in a flash when I close my eyes to remember?

That's what a dream is and that's why dreams are so special. All it takes is that one second, that one trigger and in an instant you can be back in them all over again. You can close your eyes for a moment and watch five years pass you by as if you were watching it on an old projector screen.

With one blink I can see every memory turn from blurry back into focus.

We spend all of our lives chasing our dreams. That's what we refer to as the journey. And success is a journey, not a destination, right? The journey is the adventure; it's the heart behind the chase. Trying to chase the dream and catch the dream to live it for a moment, that's the goal. To live it, to feel it, to breathe in the ray of sunshine that living the dream would give you...

All if you finally caught up to it.

The truth is that most people think that catching the dream is that picture perfect moment where you finally say I MADE IT! Or simply that end result- where the fisherman pulls his boat up to the end of the dock and holds up the giant prize fish at the end of the day and says "Caught 'em!"

What most people don't ever see, is that the chase to catch up to your dream is much more like being a really bad fisherman, not quite sure what to do in that instant when the fish finally bites down on the bait. You're so happy that you finally got the fish to bite and then the line starts to pull so you forgot that you were happy to begin with, you get completely focused on what's next and completely miss out on the happiness of that small moment.

Then, if you don't act quickly enough the line snaps and you lose out on the catch. But sometimes, if you're lucky and prepared you can reel it all in and hold onto it.

But even if you reel it in and catch it, you have another problem.

If you hold onto it for too long, you kill it.
If you let go and release it, it's gone forever.

144

And then, by the time you have decided whether to hold on or let go, you've forgotten that you caught it at all, which essentially means that you're missing out on the best part of the whole process.

Some of the greatest stories we will ever get to tell are stories of catch and release. Nothing lasts forever, but it's the story, the struggle, and the joy in getting something that makes it so worthy. No one cares about the fish if you get it handed to you at the market.

People want to know your journey; they want to know your story. Failing does not make you a failure; it actually makes you a survivor; and people need to be reminded that we all can survive.

Life isn't about getting others to follow you; life is about getting others to join you. It's about the bumps in the road and the small victories that create a trail of hope for other people to walk along. Together, we can all make a difference. Together we can encourage, together we can survive, and together we can believe.

"Don't ask what the world needs.
Ask what makes you come alive, and go do it.
Because what the world needs is people who have come
alive."

-Howard Thurman

AUTHOR'S CLOSING

Building a new chapter of my life will never negate how special every single person that was a part of Shine was and still is to me.

The choice to move on was never an easy one and the only word I can use on paper to try to explain it is *bittersweet*. It's like graduating from college, or starting a new career path, or a new chapter of your life. It's sad because you love what you had, but it's exciting because you know there can be more.

On that day, in that moment, and at that age- I made the best possible decision for Shine, the people who were a part of Shine, and for me.

I could feel the industry changing; the demographic changing, and most importantly- myself changing.

I have been asked time and time and time again if I regret it, but regret doesn't change anything.

Backspace is only a button on a keyboard. It doesn't work in real life and genuinely, I don't think I would use backspace if I could.

Do I regret it?

Very simply, no, I don't regret it. I wouldn't change it. And if I had it to do all over again, I still would have made the same decision.

If hindsight is the angel that allows you to clearly see why things happened the way they did, then regret must be the devil that sits on your shoulder and makes you question if you did the right thing to begin with.

Do I miss it?

Yes.
And let me make it very clear: Letting go and moving on will never make any part of it less meaningful.
I miss Shine desperately. I long to be back in the walls of all I had ever known. It was comfort and it was safety.

Closing the door to Shine for the last time broke my heart in so many ways, yet it grew my heart in a way full of love that I never thought I was capable of. I will never lose what I had, because it is forever in my heart to keep.

It was the perfect story, a magical span of five years in a bubble, and a real life fairytale.
You see, there's a reason why Fairytales are important for us all as we grow up. Not just because they teach us the difference between good and bad; but, more importantly, because they teach us that good always wins.

And Shine won.

Not because of trophies or placements, but because Shine is something that can forever be used as an example of hope.

Throughout these pages, I talk a lot about believing and Shine was the real life bridge between believing it and doing it.

See, for me, Shine was never the final chapter- it was the first one. And I was terrified to leave it behind because I didn't know if I could make it without that comfort and without knowing that I had that constant place to go to everyday. I always knew there was more that I wanted to do, I just didn't know if I could take that jump and actually do it.

Shine gave me so much, the greatest comfort and the strongest roots I have ever known.

But it gave me an even greater gift- a gift that I hope I can return to each and every person who ever walked through the doors of Shine.

Wings.

We all have them. Sometimes it just takes special people to remind us that they are still there. The encouragers, the believers, and the dreamers- it is those who lift others up that truly fly the highest.

There are times in life that we need time to fly and discover; to journey and to learn more about who we are and who we want to be. Sometimes it takes leaving to realize that there is no destination and as cliché as it sounds- success really is a journey.

It's terrifying not to know what comes next and it's terrifying not to have a plan. That's why most of us don't find our wings until we take the leap of faith and jump. Until we take the risk, until we take the chance, and until we rely on the belief that the wings will carry us through.

It is only then that we realize it's not the wings we need to believe in at all…

It is, very simply, ourselves.

When you give the world the best you have,
the best comes back to you.

ACKNOWLEDGEMENTS

The Letters would have never happened if it weren't for the people who were a part of the journey along the way.

Because it is the people, all of them, who taught me to forever see the good, believe in the good, and trust that the good is out there.

I am so thankful, so grateful and so humbled to have shared such a wonderful experience, to have lived a real life dream, and to have been a part of a community that always made me feel like I was at home.

These pages wouldn't exist if it weren't for the many others before me that paved the way for storytelling and had the courage to share their truth, so I would be able to share mine. I am an avid reader and many of the quotes, stories, and references throughout *The Letters* come from books I have read over the years, articles I have gotten a hold of or posts I have seen shared for the world to see.

I have been given enough inspiration to last a lifetime from those in the Cheerleading Industry.

Their stories, their victories, and their failures have all shown me that magic is real and that a community of determined individuals really can change the world.

I am forever grateful to those who I learned from, from those I have listened to, from those I have disagreed with, and from those I have united together with over the years.

It takes special people to understand how much really can happen in two minutes and thirty seconds. Years of dreams can come together and years of dreams can fall apart. Two minutes and thirty seconds is a lifetime when you're in it; and it's a split second when you're not. Two minutes and thirty seconds can be a first time, a sweet beginning, or a fresh start. Two minutes and thirty seconds can also be a bittersweet ending, a final bow, or a one last time.

We all spend so much of our lives waiting, worrying, and wishing. Two minutes and thirty seconds made me realize how precious time really is.

We're never ready for what's next. None of us. And none of us ever will be. That's why waiting is a waste of time, and when there's something you want- you can't just wait. You have to go after it, right here and right now.

And going after doesn't mean you're going to get it right away. It's not always about speed, it's about direction.
And slowing down doesn't mean you're being stopped.

The words on these pages affirm to me that it is often the road blocks and redirections that lead us to our greatest paths and bigger dreams than we've ever dreamed before.

So thank you; for the lessons, the memories, and the dreams.

And Cheers to the next two minutes and thirty seconds.

www.SomeHowItllNeverEnd.com

ABOUT THE AUTHOR

In 2007, Sydney McBride opened her own small business- a youth athletic cheerleading facility, called Shine Athletics. The business was built from the ground up as a creative vision in her head to give girls a positive place to participate in athletic activities. In 2009, she founded a Non Profit Community Fundraising event to support youth athletes and help grow the sport of cheerleading.

She is an active writer and is working on a business and leadership book titled *Building Belief.* She also plans to write a follow up memoir, detailing life after *The Letters.*

It is her hope that by sharing her story of overcoming the adversity and struggle, she can encourage young adults to believe in themselves and turn their own dreams into realities.